Changed by the King's Presence

Kurt Litwiller

Let King Jesus change you!

Kurt

Copyright © 2011 by Kurt Litwiller

All rights reserved. No part of this book may be used, reproduced, stored in a retrieval system, or transmitted in any form whatsoever — including electronic, photocopy, recording — without prior written permission from the author, except in the case of brief quotations embodied in critical articles or reviews.

All Scripture quotations, unless otherwise indicated, are taken from the Holy Bible, New International Version®. NIV®. Copyright © 1973, 1978, 1984 by International Bible Society. Used by permission of Zondervan. All rights reserved.

Edited by Michael Milligan and Janelle Litwiller

FIRST EDITION

ISBN 9780982947685

Library of Congress Control Number: 2011923505

Published by
NewBookPublishing.com, a division of Reliance Media, Inc.
2395 Apopka Blvd., #200, Apopka, FL 32703
NewBookPublishing.com

Printed in the United States of America

Dedication

This book is dedicated first and foremost to my Lord and Savior Jesus Christ. I am completely changed by the grace and love You have poured upon me. There is nothing more important to me than being in Your presence. I love to worship You and feel Your Spirit's power at work in my life.

I also dedicate this to my wife, Janelle, who stands by me in the Lord. No matter what I face, you continually keep me focused on the Lord. I am so thankful that God gave me a godly woman to spend my life with. What a blessing to have someone to seek the Lord with me. I love you!

I dedicate this also to the reader. I hope this book will be a blessing to you and help you draw closer to our God. I am not sure what you are facing today, but being in the King's presence can break down any strongholds in your life.

May God receive the glory for this book!

Table Of Contents

INTRODUCTION 7

Part 1: Ready To Meet The King

1. Approaching The King 13
2. Prepare To Meet The King 25
3. Put Yourself In A Spot To See The King 37
4. Hunger For The King 47

Part 2: Distracting Us From The King

5. The Busyness Of Life 59
6. Temptations We Face 71
7. Listening To The Wrong Voice 85
8. Caught Up In Spiritual Warfare 97
9. Thinking The Wrong Thoughts 107

Part 3: Transforming Us To Be Like The King

10. Reform Your Lives 119
11. Being Transformed 129
12. The New Nature 139
13. Be In The World—Not Of It 151
14. Our View Of Sin 163

CONCLUSION 173

Introduction

Have you ever stood in the presence of a king? Well, the United States doesn't have a king, so maybe I should rephrase that question. Have you ever stood in the presence of the President of the United States? I am not talking about being at one of his speeches or in the same room as the President. I mean being one on one with the President. Has the President ever listened intently to what you had to say? I doubt there are too many people reading this book that have been in a position like that.

Maybe we have never been in a king or President's presence like that, but we are in the Presence of our God in that way. King Jesus allows us to come and stand before Him and bring our requests to Him. We don't need a special pass to get to Him—all we need is to be washed in His blood. We all have access to the King of Kings, 24 hours a day, any day of the week.

I would truly enjoy having the opportunity to stand before the President of the United States. I would love to be able to talk with him and find out more about him than what we actually read. I know that I would be changed because of that opportunity. It would be an encounter that I would bring up in many different conversations for the rest of my life.

Being in the presence of the President would be an honor that I would never forget!

In the same way, coming before the King of Kings should be considered a great honor. It should be a time that will impact the rest of our lives. This encounter should be something that we talk about regularly in our conversations with other people. Our conversations with people, our actions, and the way we live our lives should all be affected by the encounter we had with the King who is above all Kings. Unlike the President, we can come before King Jesus every day, several times a day if we want. We have access to someone who has much more power than the President. We should never grow tired of talking to people about how we are a regular visitor before our King.

As you read this book, I want you to consider how you approach God. We would be thrilled to death and talk nonstop about meeting the President of the United States or any other famous world leader. But too often we are very nonchalant in how we come before the King of the Universe. He is just another quick conversation we whisper up quickly before we leave home, or before our meals, or before bedtime. We don't take the appropriate time to honor His Presence or engage Him deeply with a desiring heart. We approach God much like we would a phone call that we have to make and that we are happy to have end so that we can get back to the other things that we need to do for the day. Oh, but His presence should mean so much more to us than that.

Hopefully those reading this book want to know God more than they do the President of the United States.

Presidents come and go, but our King has never been dethroned, nor will He ever be. Take this journey with me and learn how to approach this Eternal King.

PART 1

Ready to Meet the King

Therefore God exalted him to the highest place and gave him the name that is above every name, that at the name of Jesus every knee should bow, in heaven and on earth and under the earth, and every tongue confess that Jesus Christ is Lord, to the glory of God the Father.
Philippians 2:9-11.

CHAPTER 1

Approaching the King

Approaching a king is serious business! There have been many people killed throughout history because they approached a king when they shouldn't have, or they approached a king with the wrong kind of attitude. Approaching the king is something we should do with humble hearts; knowing who we are in comparison with who he is. In the Bible, we see an example on how we should approach a king.

Esther was a young Jewish girl who grew up during the exile period in Israel's history. Queen Vashti, of Media/Persia, disrespected the king, so her crown was taken from her. The king searched for a new queen to take her place, and he chose Esther to be His queen. The king was unaware that his new queen was a Jewish woman. The king was convinced by one of his officials to annihilate all of the Jews. Esther, the queen, finds out that there has been a royal order to kill all of the Jews in the land. So it is up to her to approach the king on behalf of herself and her people. We see how she approaches the king in Esther 4.

⁶ So Hathach went out to Mordecai in the open square of the city in front of the king's gate. ⁷ Mordecai told him everything that had happened to him, including the exact amount of money Haman had promised to pay into the royal treasury for the destruction of the Jews. ⁸ He also gave him a copy of the text of the edict for their annihilation, which had been published in Susa, to show to Esther and explain it to her, and he told him to urge her to go into the king's presence to beg for mercy and plead with him for her people.

⁹ Hathach went back and reported to Esther what Mordecai had said. ¹⁰ Then she instructed him to say to Mordecai, ¹¹ "All the king's officials and the people of the royal provinces know that for any man or woman who approaches the king in the inner court without being summoned the king has but one law: that he be put to death. The only exception to this is for the king to extend the gold scepter to him and spare his life. But thirty days have passed since I was called to go to the king."

¹² When Esther's words were reported to Mordecai, ¹³ he sent back this answer: "Do not think that because you are in the king's house you alone of all the Jews will escape. ¹⁴ For if you remain silent at this time, relief and deliverance for the Jews will arise from

another place, but you and your father's family will perish. And who knows but that you have come to royal position for such a time as this?"

¹⁵ *Then Esther sent this reply to Mordecai:* ¹⁶ *"Go, gather together all the Jews who are in Susa, and fast for me. Do not eat or drink for three days, night or day. I and my maids will fast as you do. When this is done, I will go to the king, even though it is against the law. And if I perish, I perish."*

¹⁷ *So Mordecai went away and carried out all of Esther's instructions.*

Consecrate Yourself

I want to start by looking at the preparation required for Esther to go into the king's presence. Mordecai was Esther's cousin, but really was the father figure who raised her. He told Esther to go to the king on behalf of the Jewish people. Notice that Esther didn't agree immediately and say, "Ok, I will go talk to the king." No, she understood that even though she was the queen, there were severe consequences for approaching the king without being summoned. In verse 16, Esther says, *"Go, gather together all the Jews who are in Susa, and fast for me. Do not eat or drink for three days, night or day. I and my maids will fast as you do. When this is done, I will go to the king, even though it is against the law. And if I perish, I perish."* She knew that it was serious business to approach the king. She called for every single Jew to abstain from eating and drinking for three days. She was simply approaching an earthly king about a problem that she had—and she was the queen! Yet she approached him with humility, in awe, and in reverence. This makes me think about how we approach our Heavenly King. He is the King above all Kings. There is no power or authority greater than Him, yet too often we approach Him with no reverence or fear. We stand in the presence of the Creator of the universe, the Redeemer of our souls…and we treat that honor just like it is another routine thing we do in our day.

My wife, Janelle, and I attended a church where they served coffee, muffins, and donuts before the service. I know that there are many churches that do that, and I am not trying to pick on churches that have this ministry. But sometimes I think people come into the worship service as if they are going on a picnic in the park. I know that fasting is not something the church practices much today, but can't we go without food or drink for an hour or two a week in reverence to God? There is a time for eating before the Lord. In the Old Testament there were different feasts where they would worship before

> *We stand in the presence of the Creator of the universe, the Redeemer of our souls…and we treat that honor just like it is another rou We stand in the presence of the Creator of the universe, the Redeemer of our souls…and we treat that honor just like it is another routine thing we do in our day.*

the Lord in their eating. But there were other times when they came as a people to fast and consecrate themselves before the Lord. I know that we approach God in a different way than they did in the Old Testament, but we have completely lost the fear and awe of God.

During church services, we yawn and think to ourselves, "I have to find something to piddle with to help pass the time." We don't come prepared to meet the King. We wake up and say, "I guess I will go to church today. There is nothing else that I really need to get done today." We need to remember that we gather on Sunday morning as a people consecrated to the Lord. We gather as a community of people before the Almighty King!

It Is A Privilege To Stand Before The King

Esther knew that she did not have the right to stand in the king's presence. The only way she could stand before the king was if the king showed her grace and he held out the gold scepter to her. If he did not, she would be killed. Standing before the king was a serious matter. In verse 11, Esther says, *"All the king's officials and the people of the royal provinces know that for any man or woman who approaches the king in the inner court without being summoned the king has but one law: that he be put to death. The only exception to this is for the king to extend the gold scepter to him and spare his life. But thirty days have passed since I was called to go to the king."* Esther says here, "Everyone knows that no one can approach the king or they will be put to death." Esther, the queen, knew that approaching the king was to be done with awe and humility. How often do we approach our heavenly king with no fear or reverence...with no awe because of who He is? We are peasants standing before the king. Actually it is more than that. We are rebellious sinners coming before the King of all Kings. This chapter goes way beyond coffee and donuts, but it is about how we approach the King too casually. We yawn and think to ourselves that the service is boring today. "I can't wait to get out of here so that we can go to the Chinese restaurant." There is no awe of God in the church today. He has become our buddy, and we don't approach Him as the Holy God that He is.

Can you imagine a peasant being in the presence of a king? He wouldn't be holding a soda in one hand and a muffin in the other, wiping his mouth with his sleeve, and saying with his mouth half full, "Thank you king for seeing me." You better believe the peasant would know the holiness of being in the king's presence. He would make himself presentable, inwardly and outwardly!

We are peasants standing before the king. Actually it is more than that. We are rebellious sinners coming before the King of all Kings.

I want to make sure you comprehend this thought... It is always a peasant's privilege to stand before the king. It would be rather conceded for a peasant to think that the king was lucky to see him. "The king was blessed because I came into his presence." Unfortunately that is how a lot of people can be in their relationship with God. Too often we are so nonchalant in how we approach God that we believe that God is lucky that we came to church today to worship Him. It's as if we believe that the King of the universe wouldn't know what to do if we would have stayed home, and we actually think to ourselves, "He's got to be feeling good that I came into His presence today?" How silly! How foolish! We must see that *we* are the lucky ones that get the privilege of standing in His presence.

There have been many kings throughout history who were cruel to their own people. They treated the peasants as nobodies and would not even consider letting a peasant stand before them. Many kings were self centered, and only thought about furthering their own kingdom. They decided what was best by how it affected them, not by how it affected their people. Even with the horrible treatment the peasants would face, they would still be in awe of standing in the presence of their king.

But the King we serve is not a self seeking King. He doesn't look out for His own interests. Quite the opposite! He cared so much for us, His subjects, that He came and died upon the cross to give us an opportunity to stand in His presence. If He only cared about Himself, He would have stayed up in heaven and let us die in our sins. Yet on the cruel cross, it was just as if Jesus was holding out His gold scepter, saying, "You may enter my presence."

How are you approaching the King of Kings in your life? Are we too casual in how often, and in the manner in which, we approach the King? We come with lives that are filled with sexual immorality, un-forgiveness, filthy and lying mouths. We bring our greed and our love of money and refuse to give back to God. We satisfy our own sinful desires throughout the week and come into His presence like God owes us something for being faithful enough to come to church. We can't live our lives all week for another king, the king of this world, and then come before the King of Kings so nonchalantly. We need to remember that we are approaching the King! We should count it a privilege.

Do You Desire To Come Before The King?

Each of us needs to consider whether or not we have the desire to come before God. I don't go to church on Sunday mornings because my mom and dad make me, or because I feel like it is my duty to be at church. I don't go to see all of my friends. I go to church because it is a privilege for me to stand before the King of Kings. I could never fully explain how much I benefit from meeting with like minded Christians. You could tell me, "I will pay you five million dollars if you never go to church again." I would tell you to keep your money. I'm going before the King. Life is not about money—life is about the King. Do you get excited about going to church? If not, I think you need to take time to consider what is truly taking place in God's house.

Earlier this year, Janelle & I were on sabbatical. I was able to sit in the pews and listen to the Word of God being spoken. It

It is always a peasant's privilege to stand before the king.

ministered to my spirit. We need to be sure not to take the Word of God for granted. Psalm 119:103 says, *"How sweet are your words to my taste, sweeter than honey to my mouth!"* Many people struggle with deciding whether or not to go to church. According to the psalmist, that should not even be a question that Christians should contemplate. We should be looking at the clock anxiously, "Is it time to go yet! Is it time to enter the presence of the King? I am ready." Psalm 122:1 says, *"I rejoiced with those who said to me, 'let us go to the house of the Lord.'"* Put yourself in a position to see and hear God.

People show what is important to them by their desire to be there on time. People will make sure to get to an interview on time, but when it comes to standing before the King…five, ten, fifteen minutes late is not that big of a deal. If you were standing before the king, would you tell him, "I only have one hour to give you, then I have to leave?" Sporting events can go into overtime with hardly any complaints, but if church isn't over in an hour, they get restless and irritated.

Once you have truly stood in the presence of the king, you can't wait to be back in His presence again. A peasant would be honored each time to be in a king's presence, even if he had that privilege ten times a week. A peasant would never get tired of it, or think to himself, "I would be better off to stay at home today instead of going before the king." That is never the case. It is never a mistake to come to church and listen to God's Word being spoken; and to lift up the praises of God.

Often there are Christians that go home from church and say that they didn't get anything out of the worship service. I feel sorry for them, because each time I leave church, I know I have been in the presence of the King of Kings. The preacher might not have preached the best sermon, but I know God's promise…His Word will not return to Him void. He will minister to us no matter how bad the sermon was, or how many mistakes there were when the praise team was leading the songs. Those who truly understand that they are in the presence of the King will leave a changed person, because they know they have experienced the King's presence.

It's Your Time To Come Before The King

Esther was hesitant to go into the king's presence. Mordecai tried to encourage her to go before the king. In Esther 4:14 it says, *"For if you remain silent at this time, relief and deliverance for the Jews will arise from another place, but you and your father's family will perish. And who knows but that you have come to royal position for such a time as this?"* Mordecai was saying, "You are where you are for a purpose. It is not an accident that you are the Queen at this time in history. You are queen so you can save yourself and your people. Esther, it is time to approach the king." I would like to echo Mordecai's words today. "You are where you are for a purpose. It is no accident that you are

> *Yet on the cruel cross, it was like Jesus was holding out His gold scepter saying, "You may enter my presence."*

reading this book. Today is the day you are to approach King Jesus."

The situation is the same for us today. We do not deserve to come into the presence of our King. We deserve death because of our sins. We deserve the eternal fires of hell. But King Jesus went to the cross and took upon Himself all of our shame and all of our sins. Because of the cross, the King of Kings stands ready to hold out the gold scepter to you so that you can enter His presence. We never need to wonder if today is the day that we can go to Him. We are always welcome to enter His presence.

Maybe as you read this, you realize your need for this King. Come to Him and receive His salvation. Only this King can give you eternal life. Others of you may be convicted about how casually you approach the King of Kings. Lay your heart open before Him. Who knows, maybe you are reading this today, for such a time as this!

> *Lord Jesus,*
>
> *We recognize You as King. We see that You are the King above all Kings! There is no power equal to You or above You. Lord, I realize that I am a peasant, covered in my filthy rags of sin. I deserve hell because of my sin against You. Yet, I thank You for the cross of Jesus that makes it possible for me to stand in Your presence. You welcome me each and every time I come to You. Lord, help me not to take this privilege for granted. Help me see*

the extreme privilege it is to have the King's undivided attention whenever I call. Lord, I approach You with awe and wonder for who You are, and for Your mighty grace that cares for a peasant like me. I humbly bow my knee, and my life to the glory of my King. In Jesus' name, Amen.

CHAPTER 2

Prepare To Meet The King

This is hard for me to share because I am a Cubs fan, but Sammy Sosa (right fielder for the Cubs many years ago) was kicked out of a baseball game because it was discovered that he had used a corked bat. He'd hit a ball, the bat broke, and there was the embarrassing evidence that the bat he was using was illegal. Sosa apologized to the fans after the game and said he simply picked up the wrong bat. The league announced that it had examined all 70 of his other bats and all of them were "legit." For those who don't know what it means to have a corked bat, some hitters drill out the core of a hardwood bat and fill it with cork. This results in the bat retaining its hitting power, while at the same time, becoming lighter and easier to swing. Sosa says he only uses a corked bat in homerun contests and during batting practices. The fans love to see him hit the long ball, he said. Bottom line: Sosa's bat looked the same as everyone else's, but it had cork inside of it. You couldn't tell it was corked by looking at the outside.[1]

In this chapter we are going to focus on the fact that what is inside of us is of the utmost importance. It is not the external appearance that matters. Sometimes we try to hide what is inside of us…but like Sammy Sosa's bat, sooner or later people will see what's inside. We see in 1 Samuel 16 that God cares more about the inside of us, than the outside.

> [1] *The LORD said to Samuel, "How long will you mourn for Saul, since I have rejected him as king over Israel? Fill your horn with oil and be on your way; I am sending you to Jesse of Bethlehem. I have chosen one of his sons to be king."*
> [2] *But Samuel said, "How can I go? Saul will hear about it and kill me."*
> *The LORD said, "Take a heifer with you and say, 'I have come to sacrifice to the LORD.'* [3] *Invite Jesse to the sacrifice, and I will show you what to do. You are to anoint for me the one I indicate."*
> [4] *Samuel did what the LORD said. When he arrived at Bethlehem, the elders of the town trembled when they met him. They asked, "Do you come in peace?"*
> [5] *Samuel replied, "Yes, in peace; I have come to sacrifice to the LORD. Consecrate yourselves and come to the sacrifice with me." Then he consecrated Jesse and his sons and invited them to the sacrifice.*
> [6] *When they arrived, Samuel saw Eliab and thought, "Surely the LORD's anointed stands here before the LORD."*

⁷ But the LORD said to Samuel, "Do not consider his appearance or his height, for I have rejected him. The LORD does not look at the things man looks at. Man looks at the outward appearance, but the LORD looks at the heart."

⁸ Then Jesse called Abinadab and had him pass in front of Samuel. But Samuel said, "The LORD has not chosen this one either." ⁹ Jesse then had Shammah pass by, but Samuel said, "Nor has the LORD chosen this one." ¹⁰ Jesse had seven of his sons pass before Samuel, but Samuel said to him, "The LORD has not chosen these." ¹¹ So he asked Jesse, "Are these all the sons you have?"

"There is still the youngest," Jesse answered, "but he is tending the sheep."

Samuel said, "Send for him; we will not sit down until he arrives."

¹² So he sent and had him brought in. He was ruddy, with a fine appearance and handsome features.

Then the LORD said, "Rise and anoint him; he is the one."

¹³ So Samuel took the horn of oil and anointed him in the presence of his brothers, and from that day on the Spirit of the LORD came upon David in power. Samuel then went to Ramah.

Prepare Yourself To Worship

God told Samuel to go to Bethlehem and to invite Jesse & his sons to a sacrifice. Samuel was going to Bethlehem because he was going to anoint the next king. Samuel listened to the Lord and he traveled to Bethlehem. When Samuel arrived, he told the elders in verse 5. *"Consecrate yourselves and come to the sacrifice with me."* Consecrating yourself means to prepare oneself both physically and spiritually. It would involve going home, getting cleaned up, and getting your mind focused on the Lord. Preparing yourself to come before the Lord. I often wonder how many church going people come prepared to meet the Lord. I'm not just talking about taking a shower and combing their hair, but taking the time to get their mind focused on God. Prepare to hear His Word. Too often I think we are out late the night before church, and we are so tired that we are not very alert during the service the next day. Or we might have rolled out of bed just in time to get to church. We have it down pat—we know exactly what time we have to get up to make it to church. "I have to get up at 9:40 to eat, shower, and allow five minutes to get to church—just to slip in the church by 10:30." People rush to prepare themselves physically for church, but give no thought to preparing themselves spiritually. There are others that watch TV shows on Sunday mornings which do not help get their minds focused on meeting with the Lord. We need to prepare ourselves to meet with God; prepare to hear from God.

If we had a test at school or a project to present at

work, we would make sure we were in bed at a decent hour so we could get plenty of rest. We would look over our notes in the morning for some last minute preparation. It may sound silly, but for church we need to get a good night's rest and wake up thumbing through God's Word. So the question is, when we come together on Sunday morning, what do you do in preparation for meeting God?

Some people say, "The preacher didn't say anything I needed to hear today." It is more likely that they didn't prepare themselves to hear what God wanted them to hear today. I don't care how bad the preacher is, if he is speaking God's Word—there is something for everyone to hear. In 1 Kings 19, God did not speak to Elijah in the earthquake, or the thunder, or the fire, or the huge wind—but God chose to speak to Elijah in a gentle whisper. Many people miss what God wants to tell them because they are not prepared to hear the small whisper of God. This is an important point for two reasons. First, if we don't prepare ourselves we will miss out on something that God wants to tell us. Secondly, we are not giving God the worship that He deserves. We can't open our hearts to God like we should if we have been arguing with our spouse or kids all morning long. God deserves better than our coming into church sleepy, singing, "(YAAAAAAAWN) I praise you Lord." God deserves a congregation that is alert and focused on Him—bringing Him the praise that He deserves.

> *If you are tired or not focused on God, you will not be alert enough to pick up the things God wants to teach you.*

God Is More Concerned About The Inside

Samuel was in Bethlehem looking for the next king to take the place of King Saul. King Saul was an impressive man. The Bible says he stood a head taller than anyone else. No wonder Saul was king, it was natural for people to follow someone who looked so impressive. Samuel knew the next king was going to be one of Jesse's sons, but he didn't know which one. So he had each of them pass in front of him. Eliab, the first son, came and stood before Samuel. Samuel thought to himself, "This is the one that the Lord would have me anoint. Look at him—he is an impressive man—he is the oldest...surely the Lord would have him as king." But in 1 Samuel 16:7 we read, *"But the Lord said to Samuel, 'Do not consider his appearance or his height, for I have rejected him. The Lord does not look at the things man looks at. Man looks at the outward appearance, but the Lord looks at the heart.'"* The Lord was not impressed with Eliab's physical appearance like Samuel was. The Lord was more concerned about the condition of his heart—what kind of a leader he would be. It doesn't matter if you look like a leader, what really matters is that you have the qualities of a leader. I mentioned that King Saul was an impressive man, but he didn't obey the Lord. God is more concerned about finding someone who will follow Him and less interested in their intelligence or physical stature.

Jesse had all but one of his sons pass before Samuel, but the Lord didn't choose any of them. It is interesting that David was not even considered important enough to be at the sacrifice. He is the youngest and the smallest. Yet he is the one that the Lord chose. This is a message that our world needs to hear because we are too focused on appearances. We are exactly like Samuel. We see someone and we immediately have an opinion about that person just by the way they look. You may say, "I'm too much of a Christian to judge people by the way they look." Well Samuel was a prophet of God and even he made the mistake of judging by appearances. We need to really watch ourselves. Things are not always what they seem.

> There was a man who saw an advertisement for a job at the zoo. When he went there, he was horrified to find that the only job they had open was for somebody to play the part of a monkey. A lot of children were coming in the next few days, and the zoo, having no monkeys, needed someone to impersonate one. Since money was tight, the man decided he would take the job. He arrived before sunrise, got into the monkey outfit, and slipped into his cage. Finally, day dawned, and the children came. All he had to do was pace the floor, swing from tree to tree, and eat bananas whenever they were fed to him. After eight or ten hours, he became thoroughly exhausted. As he swung from one tree to another, he slipped and fell into the lion's den next door. He shouted, "Help! Help!" The lion quickly

ran over to where the man was and said, "If you don't be quiet, we'll both lose our jobs."[2]

That is kind of a silly story, but the point is a good one; you can fool people with your appearance. What's inside can be completely different than what's on the outside. The old saying is true, "You can't judge a book by its cover." The book could have a fancy cover but be the worst, boring book you have ever read. And another book could have a plain cover but be the best, most exciting book you have ever read. You have to open up the book and read it before you know how good it is. It's the same way when we look at people. We can't know a person by their appearances. There are people who look a little rough around the edges, but they know God and love other people, and they wouldn't hurt anybody. And then, there are clean cut people whose hearts are actually really perverse. It doesn't matter how they have their haircut or what type of clothing they wear. What matters the most is their hearts. God is more concerned about the heart than He is the hairdo.

I want you to think about something. How many hours did you spend getting ready this week? Think about all of the time you spent showering, shaving, brushing your teeth, combing your hair, and putting on make-up. You probably spend more hours doing that than you think. Now let me ask you, how many hours did you spend reading the Bible, praying, and

God is more concerned about the heart than He is the hairdo.

meditating on God? Did you spend more time preparing your body, or your spirit for the day? Could you imagine if we would wake up in the morning and spend only five minutes getting ready for the day? Wow, we would probably look like a mess. That is how we are spiritually! We spend five minutes, if that, getting ready spiritually for the battles that we will have to face that day. And spiritually our lives are a mess! Something needs to change. We are obsessed with the way that we look, and not very concerned at all about seeking out God.

Jesus says in Luke 11:39-40, *"Now then, you Pharisees clean the outside of the cup and dish, but inside you are full of greed and wickedness. You foolish people! Did not the one who made the outside make the inside also?"* The inside of a man, the heart and inner righteousness, is more important than the outside. We can wash the outside, but the inside can still be dirty. Think about the illustration Jesus shared of the cup and the dish. Which would you rather have clean, the inside or outside? God is saying that we are that dish. We clean the outside (bodies), but we overlook cleaning the inside (our hearts).

People will do a lot of things to change their appearance. They will starve themselves to lose weight, they will buy expensive things to make themselves look good, and they even have plastic surgery to get rid of what they see as flaws. When you pick up a magazine or turn on the TV, you will see that the world measures you by the way you look. People are getting rich by introducing diet plans, hair replacements, work out tapes; because people are so concerned with what their body looks like. There is no way we can dress in cheap clothes or have cheap possessions. We must have the best. Instead of buying the $15 jeans on sale, we want the designer jeans that cost $80. We have to have the newest fashions so that we can look good.

Some people will be impressed by the way you look. If you are out for the praise of man you can obtain it. But what matters to God is the attitude of your heart. Are you the same person at home by yourself that you are when you are in public?

> *We spend 5 minutes, if that, getting ready spiritually for the battles that we will have to face that day. And spiritually our lives are a mess.*

The measure of a man's real character is what he would do if he knew no one would find out. We look in the mirror to make sure we look OK. Hair is combed, nothing on our face, lipstick and mascara looks good. We are continually concerned with our appearance, but we need to continually look in the mirror of God's Word. Am I gossiping about someone, or greedy with my money? Am I going out of my way to help people who need it? Am I living a sexually pure life? I challenge you today to start working more on your inward appearance.

People are not going to be attracted to the church because of our physical appearance. People will be drawn to a church because they display the loving qualities of Jesus. It is the fruit of the Spirit that we have working in our lives that will make us attractive to the world. God is still looking for people who have a heart seeking after Him. Start today by being more concerned about your appearance before God, than you are with your appearance before man.

CHAPTER 3

Put Yourself In A Spot To See The King

There was an experiment in which kids were divided into two groups. One group was given a puzzle to put together, but they didn't give the kids the box top that had the picture of what the puzzle would look like when they were done. The kids jumped in with excitement, but quickly became frustrated when they couldn't figure out how the pieces where suppose to fit together—so they quit. Then they gave another group of kids the exact same puzzle, but this time they gave them the box top with the picture on it. The kids sat down and had a blast putting it together. They saw how all the pieces fit together.[3]

Well, think of life as a puzzle. Sometimes pieces of our lives make no sense at all; we don't know how all these pieces are supposed to fit together. Often people become unmotivated in life or get frustrated and quit. But if we have Jesus in our lives, we can understand how some of those pieces are suppose to fit together. Puzzles can be hard to put together, but the box makes it easier. Life can be hard to make sense of, but we have a guide that makes it easier—The

Bible. In Luke 19, we see someone who starts to understand the puzzle of his life a little more clearly.

> [1] *Jesus entered Jericho and was passing through.* [2] *A man was there by the name of Zacchaeus; he was a chief tax collector and was wealthy.* [3] *He wanted to see who Jesus was, but being a short man he could not, because of the crowd.* [4] *So he ran ahead and climbed a sycamore-fig tree to see him, since Jesus was coming that way.*
>
> [5] *When Jesus reached the spot, he looked up and said to him, "Zacchaeus, come down immediately. I must stay at your house today."* [6] *So he came down at once and welcomed him gladly.*
>
> [7] *All the people saw this and began to mutter, "He has gone to be the guest of a 'sinner.'"*
>
> [8] *But Zacchaeus stood up and said to the Lord, "Look, Lord! Here and now I give half of my possessions to the poor, and if I have cheated anybody out of anything, I will pay back four times the amount."*
>
> [9] *Jesus said to him, "Today salvation has come to this house, because this man, too, is a son of Abraham.* [10] *For the Son of Man came to seek and to save what was lost."*

Put Yourself In A Position To See Jesus

Let me set up this scene. Just before this passage Jesus was approaching the town of Jericho. He was still on the outskirts of town and He came upon a blind man. Jesus restored this blind man's sight in full view of everyone around. Now, as we pick up this passage, it is just minutes after He healed this blind man. It says, Jesus is now entering Jericho, and like always, there is a crowd around Him. People had just seen Him heal the blind man, so they were flocking to Him. Everyone wanted to touch Him, to talk to Him, just be next to Him. If you saw Jesus heal somebody, wouldn't you want to join in the crowd to see what He was going to do next? Everyone wanted to see Jesus because they had heard that He could do amazing things.

I can picture a wall of people all around Jesus. Fifty, or even hundreds of people surrounding Jesus. Zacchaeus, being a short man, couldn't see Jesus because of the crowd. How desperately he wanted to see Jesus!

There was an obstacle between him and Jesus. But he wanted to see Jesus bad enough that he came up with a plan to remove the obstacle.

There was an obstacle between him and Jesus. But he wanted to see Jesus bad enough that he came up with a plan to remove the obstacle. He ran ahead of the crowd and climbed a sycamore tree. And when Jesus passed that way, Zacchaeus was high enough above the crowd that he could see this Jesus who he so desperately wanted to see.

I want to pause right here in this story to say, there

may be people reading this today that feel like Zacchaeus. They have some type of obstacle in their way from getting a good look at Jesus. I am not talking about them being short and unable to see Jesus, but for some reason their view of Jesus is blocked or is limited because of some obstacle in their life. My first question to them is, "How bad do you want to see Jesus?" If we want to see Jesus as bad as Zacchaeus did, we can find a way. We all have obstacles in our lives that try to wedge their way in between us and Jesus. This world wants to separate us from Him. They don't want us to get a good look at our Savior. Some obstacles the world puts in our way are bitterness, jealousy, and materialism. If the world gets us caught up in these things, it is hard for us to be able to see Jesus. Maybe we are just too busy looking at other things in our lives to have that deep desire to see Jesus at any cost.

It would have been so easy for Zacchaeus to say, "Well I guess I can't catch a glimpse of Jesus today, the crowd is too big." He could have gone home with his life unchanged. But he was determined; no obstacle was going to stop him from seeing Jesus. Are you at the same point as Zacchaeus? Are you willing to do whatever you have to do? Are you willing to push all obstacles aside just to see Him? Are you willing to push aside the bitterness you have for your neighbor? To push aside the jealousy you feel that the Jones' have a bigger house? To put aside the bad behaviors in your life that are holding you back from seeing Jesus clearly? Zacchaeus sure found it worthwhile.

There may be people reading this who don't go to church on a regular basis. You are discouraged in your faith and you wonder why you don't experience God like other people do. It's because you need to be like Zacchaeus and put yourself in a place where you can experience Him. I know God is capable of meeting you in your bed on Sunday morning, but I think He is more likely to meet with you where a number of believers are gathered to lift up praises to Him. Does God see a desire in your heart to meet with Him? Put yourself in a place to see God. Zaccheaus didn't just go home to sit in his easy chair, he ran ahead of the crowd and climbed a tree.

> *I am ready to tear down all obstacles in my life that limit my view of Jesus. If you do that, I think you will see it is worthwhile.*

Jesus Is The One Who Invites Us To Be With Him

Zacchaeus put himself in a spot to see Jesus, but it was Jesus who gave the invitation to be in a relationship. The Bible tells us that it is the Spirit who brings us into a relationship with God. We don't draw ourselves closer to God on our own. Zaccheaus was climbing the tree just to catch a glimpse of Jesus—and he could do that on his own. But he got more than a glimpse. His life was changed because of Jesus' invitation to have a relationship with Him. Jesus said to Zacchaeus, *"Come down immediately. I must stay at your house today."* Jesus chose to use strong words here. "I must stay at your house." In Biblical times, no matter who you were, or how popular you were, you would never invite yourself into someone else's house. But Jesus did this so that

He could accomplish what He was sent to do. Verse 10 tells us His mission, *"For the Son of Man came to seek and to save what was lost."* Jesus' invitation here is for everyone. Look at who Zaccheaus is. It says in verse 2 that he was a chief tax collector. Tax collectors were considered great sinners because they would overcharge people and make lots of money for themselves. So a chief tax collector takes it to a greater scale—he was one of the top tax collectors in the business. So people not only saw Zaccheaus as a sinner, but a huge sinner. Surely Jesus would not be interested in someone like this. But that is what Jesus came to this earth for; He came to rescue sinners. You may think you are too big of a sinner to be forgiven. But that is not the case. I don't care how bad your life has been up to this point, what matters is what you do from this point on. You've messed up…join the club—I'm at the top of that list. But today can be a new start.

In the 1929 Rose Bowl game, Georgia Tech was playing the University of California. Right before half time a player recovered a fumble, but became confused and ran the wrong way. A teammate tackled him just before he would have scored a touchdown for the other team. At half time all of the players went into the dressing room and sat down, wondering

I don't care how bad your life has been up to this point, what matters is what you do from this point on.

what the coach would say. This young man sat by himself; put a towel over his head, and cried. The coach didn't say anything about the play during his halftime speech. When the team was ready to go back onto the field for the second half, the coach stunned the team when he announced that the same players who started the first half would start the second half. All of the players left the dressing room except this young man. He wouldn't budge. The coach looked back as he called him again, and saw his cheeks were wet with tears. The player said, "Coach, I can't do it. I've ruined you. I've disgraced the University of California. I can't face the crowd in the stadium again." Then the coach put his hand on the players shoulder and said, "Get up and go back in there. The game is only half way over."[4]

I can see God as the coach in that image, lovingly placing His hand on you, "Yes you have made some mistakes in the first half of your life, but your life is not over yet. I have confidence in you. Shake off your mistakes and do the best that you can do from here on out." There is no question that we are sinners and we don't deserve mercy. But Jesus came down to die on the cross, making it possible for you to be forgiven of your sins and to become a friend of God.

It's Up To Us To Respond

Jesus saw Zacchaeus up in the tree and told him to come down, because He wanted to spend time with him. The ball was then in Zaccheaus' court. He could have said, "I just wanted to see you. I have seen you, now I am satisfied. All I wanted to do was see you; I wasn't asking for you to come into my life and change it around. Slow down Jesus!" But Zacchaeus wanted Jesus to come to his home. He came down immediately. He didn't think about it, "Should I have Jesus come to my house or not?" He didn't contemplate it for five minutes. He knew he wanted Jesus to go home with him.

Look at Zaccheaus' response to Jesus in verse 8, *"Look, Lord! Here and now I give half of my possessions to the poor, and if I have cheated anybody out of anything, I will pay back four times the amount."* Zacchaeus was no longer going to overcharge people because his life was changed. When Jesus is our Lord, it changes the way we relate to people around us. When we encounter Jesus, we want to make things right. We admit that we have done things wrong and have a desire to make things right. It changes the way we treat people.

I stand amazed that Jesus took notice of this one man when He was surrounded by a crowd of people. But you can see why He did. Zacchaeus put himself in a position to see God. Matthew 5:6 says, *"Blessed are those who hunger and thirst for*

> *Now that Jesus is my Lord it changes the way I relate to people around me. When we encounter Jesus, we want to make things right.*

righteousness, for they will be filled." If you want to know more of God, if you pursue the things of God…He will show Himself to you. His desire is to be in a relationship with you. Just like Zacchaeus, Jesus wants to go home with you today. You may not be sitting up in a tree, but you are reading this book to get a better view of Jesus. Jesus wants to speak to you individually today. "Take me home, I can change your life." Don't just settle for a glimpse.

CHAPTER 4

Hunger For The King

Cast Away is a movie about a character named Chuck Noland (Tom Hanks), who is a top engineer for FedEx. While flying over the South Pacific, a violent storm damages the company jet causing it to slam into the ocean. Noland survives the crash, but everyone else aboard is killed. Clinging to a yellow life raft, he rides out the raging storm and is washed up on a small deserted island. For the next four years he struggles to survive before escaping the island and returning to civilization. The day after Noland first sets foot on the island, the only concern greater than his fear is his desperate need for water. He is dangerously thirsty. After he discovers the coconuts falling from the trees, Noland frantically attempts to open one. He repeatedly throws a coconut against a boulder, but the hard shell is unmarked. Using all his strength, he pounds the coconut with a rock, but he has no success. He tries to drill a hole into one and then flies into a fury when he still cannot access the juice locked inside the fibrous seed. Eventually he employs a sharp rock as an axe and is able to cut into and remove the outer husk. Left with the hard shell, he finally breaks it open only to watch as most of the milky juice spills out on the ground. Noland lifts up a fragment of the shell and drains the few remaining drops of liquid into his mouth.[5]

Noland went through a lot of work to get a few drops of liquid. Do we have a thirst like that to know more about our King? We need to dig and dig into the Word of God. We need to diligently seek God in prayer. We need to fellowship with other believers just to get a "few drops" more of God. We should be so thirsty for God that we will do whatever we need to do, to get our thirst quenched. We see in Matthew 15 that there is a woman who had a true desire for Jesus. She was desperate even for a "few drops" of what Jesus had to offer.

> [21] *Leaving that place, Jesus withdrew to the region of Tyre and Sidon.* [22] *A Canaanite woman from that vicinity came to him, crying out, "Lord, Son of David, have mercy on me! My daughter is suffering terribly from demon-possession."*
>
> [23] *Jesus did not answer a word. So his disciples came to him and urged him, "Send her away, for she keeps crying out after us."*
>
> [24] *He answered, "I was sent only to the lost sheep of Israel."*
>
> [25] *The woman came and knelt before him. "Lord, help me!" she said.*
>
> [26] *He replied, "It is not right to take the children's bread and toss it to their dogs."*

^{27} *"Yes, Lord,"* she said, *"but even the dogs eat the crumbs that fall from their masters' table."*

^{28} Then Jesus answered, *"Woman, you have great faith! Your request is granted."* And her daughter was healed from that very hour.

Children's Rejection Of The Bread

Just before this passage, Jesus was teaching the religious leaders about what makes them clean and unclean. The whole discussion came about because the disciples ate food with unwashed hands. Jesus said that people are not unclean because they eat with dirty hands. People are unclean because of what comes out of their heart. The religious elite thought they were justified by God by observing strict laws that they made up. Jesus makes it clear that it is your heart (inner character) that makes you acceptable before God.

As we transition into this passage, the scene shifts but the topic is still the same. Jesus leaves the people of Israel and now stands before someone who is considered to be unclean; a foreigner. Jesus was approached by a Gentile woman. She wanted Jesus to heal her daughter. Jesus answered her in verse 24, *"I was sent only to the lost sheep of Israel."* It seems to me that in this passage Jesus doesn't want anything to do with this Gentile woman. But we see in the Bible that Jesus healed many other Gentile people with no questions asked. I think Jesus was trying to make a point here. We know He cares for all people regardless of nationality. He had just finished teaching the religious leaders that the only thing that matters is the heart—that it doesn't matter about religious ceremonies, how much money you give, or from what nationality you come from. But we do see that Jesus' first priority was to the people of Israel. The time would come soon enough for the door to be opened to the Gentiles. Jesus was interested in the Jews because the salvation that He was bringing came from the Jewish faith. He was coming to the Jews to fulfill their law, and once the law was fulfilled, then all people have the means of being saved. So it is not that Jesus has no concern for the Gentiles, He is just trying to give priority to Israel. They are the children of God and they received the teachings and blessings first.

After the woman continues to ask for help, Jesus answers in verse 26, *"It is not right to take the children's bread and toss it to their dogs."* You would not take food out of your child's hand so that you could feed your dog. Your first priority would be your child, but children often do not want the food that you make for them. Kids will not eat certain things because they tend to be too picky. The family dog loves it when kids reject food because they suddenly become the beneficiaries. Jesus came to Israel, but His people did not want to receive the bread He had to offer them. Jesus is the "bread of heaven", but they rejected Him. The Gentiles are there to receive the "bread of heaven", with open arms.

Matthew 5:6 says, *"Blessed are those who hunger and thirst for righteousness, for they will be filled."*

We need to make sure that we are not so picky that we refuse to receive all that God has to give us. The Jewish people could have been in a much better position if they would have just received their King when He came to them. Too often we also reject the bread God wants to give us because we want the tempting bread that the world has to offer us. The world offers us bread that looks good. It is pleasurable, it is immediate, and it tastes good on the tongue. But unfortunately, it spoils quickly once we swallow it. God's bread is true, it is eternal, and it is worth the wait. We need to receive the bread of God's Word and not desire the temporary pleasures of the world.

The Only Desire Of Dogs Is To Get The Crumbs

In verse 27 the woman replies to Jesus, *"Yes, Lord, but even the dogs eat the crumbs that fall from their masters' table."* This woman recognized that Jesus is a Jewish teacher, the Jewish Messiah sent for His people. She knew He was going to take care of His own people first. But she just asked for crumbs. This woman recognized her role in faith, and she was fine with it. She says, "I'm not asking for what belongs to others, but please give me what falls to the ground." For those of you who have dogs, you know when you eat that they stay close by the table—and they are ready to pounce on anything that hits the floor. They are not as picky as your kids who sit at the table. The dogs don't care if it is chicken, turkey, hamburger…whatever falls is going to be eaten. I've been to some people's houses where the little kids can't seem to find their mouth, in which most of the food ends up on the floor. The dog probably gets more to eat than the kids do. Or maybe the kids don't like the food so they sneak it on the floor for the dog.

In Jesus' ministry, there were a lot of crumbs. The religious rulers did not want to accept Jesus and His teachings. The Gentiles were right there to say, "We will take what they don't want." You can see the contrast between the Jews and the Gentiles. Jesus <u>went</u> to the Jews to give them the good news, but they rejected it. While the Gentiles <u>came to Jesus</u> desiring to receive Him & His teachings.

A crumb from heaven that is on the earth is greater than a great feast here on earth. Give me a crumb of heaven, and I will be glad to sacrifice all of these earthly things that I have. My in-laws have a dog named Brecky. He could have a bowl full of food waiting to be eaten, but if you sit down at the table to eat, he will be right there waiting for any little thing to fall. He would rather have a crumb from our table than a bowl full of his food. He is right there to catch the bacon you drop before it hits the floor.

> *A crumb from heaven on the earth is greater than a great feast here on earth. Give me a crumb of heaven, and I will be glad to sacrifice all these earthly things that I have.*

Can't we see that we should be the same way? We should be waiting on God's goodness instead of being caught up in the food of this world. Just a crumb from the banqueting table of the King of Kings is better than any feast this world can offer you.

Potato chips, cheese curls, and candy may be some of your favorite things to eat, but for a few mule deer in Arizona's Grand Canyon National Park, these foods proved to be deadly. Park rangers had to kill over two dozen mule deer because they became hooked on junk food left by visitors to the park. Once they get a taste of the sugar and salt, the deer develop an extreme addiction and will go to any lengths to eat only junk food. This results in the animals ignoring the food they need, leaving them in poor health and on the edge of starvation. Because of junk food cravings, the deer lose their natural ability to digest vegetation. One park ranger called the junk food "the crack cocaine of the deer world." Scripture warns us of the dangers of developing a craving for the things of this world. Such a diet keeps us from hungering for the things of God.[6]

Some people are very content with their bowl full of food on earth. They care nothing for the things of God, saying, "I don't want anything from His table." While others forsake what they have here on earth and completely focus on God. Some people are just waiting to catch a crumb of God's truth that falls their way. They don't care about the big house, the fancy cars, the prestigious careers—they want to make sure they are at a place where they can receive crumbs from heaven.

Matthew 5:6 says, *"Blessed are those who hunger and thirst for righteousness, for they will be filled."* He wants to feed you more truth about Himself. He wants to have a closer relationship with you. He is ready to give you more of Himself, if you just ask. I know a lot of people with dogs that feed them from the table. They see their dogs sitting quietly beside the table, earnestly focused on them and it breaks their heart. They throw their best friend a little piece of meat to give them a little taste. I see God in the same way. When we come and quietly seek Him out, and wait upon Him—He is glad to throw us a little bit of His truth to us. God is not up in heaven at His banqueting table, making sure nothing falls to the ground for us. He doesn't have such a tight hold on His blessings that we can't even pry them out of His hands. No, God is wanting to pour His blessings out on the ones that love Him and seek Him. Remember this promise in Matthew 5:6, if you hunger and thirst for God He will fill you. He will drop crumbs all over earth if He sees that we are interested in them.

> *Someday we will have more than crumbs. Someday we will actually be at the banqueting table of God.*

Someday we will have more than crumbs. Someday we will actually be at the banqueting table of God. We won't have a crumb of God's truth, we will actually be looking at the "Truth". But until then, as we walk upon this earth—don't get too focused on our bowl full of earthly possessions. Our possessions, our money, our health—they will all pass away.

But the crumbs we receive from heaven are just a sample of the great things that are yet to come!

PART 2

Distracting Us From The King

Timothy, guard what has been entrusted to your care. Turn away from godless chatter and the opposing ideas of what is falsely called knowledge, which some have professed and in so doing have wandered from the faith. Grace be with you.
                              1 Timothy 6:20-21

CHAPTER 5

The Busyness Of Life

Have you ever seen a lion trainer going into a lion's cage? They have their whips, and their pistols are at their sides. But they also carry a stool. What good is a stool going to do against a huge lion? But trainers say that the stool is the most important tool they have. They hold the stool by the seat and thrust the legs of the stool toward the face of the wild animal. The Lion tries to focus on all four legs at once. In the attempt to focus on all four, the animal becomes paralyzed. It becomes tame, weak because its attention is fragmented.[7]

We can be a lot like the lion. We can get so focused on all of the things that are coming at us that we become paralyzed. Instead of spending time in God's Word and taking the time to pray to Him, we find our energy going towards thinking about all that is going on in our lives. Have you ever felt that way? Your mind is so consumed by the worries of the day, that they just paralyze you until those problems are solved. Soon after those problems are solved, we have new worries that consume our thoughts. We need to stop being distracted by all the stuff life throws at us. In Luke 10, we see how easily it is to get distracted.

[38] *As Jesus and his disciples were on their way, he came to a village where a woman named Martha opened her home to him.* [39] *She had a sister called Mary, who sat at the Lord's feet listening to what he said.* [40] *But Martha was distracted by all the preparations that had to be made. She came to him and asked, "Lord, don't you care that my sister has left me to do the work by myself? Tell her to help me!"*
[41] *"Martha, Martha," the Lord answered, "you are worried and upset about many things,* [42] *but only one thing is needed. Mary has chosen what is better, and it will not be taken away from her."*

Martha's Serving Attitude

Verse 38 starts out by saying, *"As Jesus and his disciples were on their way, he came to a village..."* We know from the last chapter, Luke 9:51, that Jesus was on His way to Jerusalem. The disciples never knew where they were going to be from night to night. They followed Jesus and they stopped wherever He did. They didn't have a long agenda saying, "Thursday night we will stop in this city, and Friday we will stop in this city, and Saturday we will arrive in Jerusalem." So coming to Martha & Mary's house probably was not a scheduled stop. They were passing through, and Martha, out of the kindness of her heart, invited them into her house.

All of a sudden, Martha has 13 guests that she has to feed (Jesus and the 12 disciples). So, like thousands of hosts and hostesses around the world, Martha started a frenzy of activity in order to feed her guests. Martha could not order fast food or go out to a restaurant. They had no Pizza Hut or Papa John's to call for delivery. There were no freezers to pull out frozen hamburger patties to cook. Think of the last minute preparation that Martha had to make. She probably had to grind up some flour to make bread. She probably had to kill and cook a chicken. She probably had to get water from the town well because it wouldn't have been pumped to her house like it is for us today. She would have to set the table. And more than likely, like most of us when we invite guests over, she had to straighten up the house to make it look presentable for her guests.

While Martha was doing all this work, she saw Mary just sitting and talking to Jesus. And that was when Martha lost it. I can just see Martha snapping. In verse 40, Martha says, *"Lord, don't you care that my sister has left me to do the work by myself? Tell her to help me!"* I can see the anger and frustration in Martha, "I am working my fingers to the bone, and my sister is over there doing nothing!" Martha went into the room where Jesus was, and she didn't rebuke her sister in front of Jesus, but instead, she pointed out the injustice of the situation. She almost seemed to rebuke Jesus for not caring, for not ordering Mary to go help her. She seems to be commanding Jesus, "Tell her to help me!" The way in which this is phrased in the Greek language shows us that Martha was expecting a positive response from Jesus, such as, "Martha, you're right. Mary you better get up and help her." There was no doubt in Martha's mind that her work was extremely important and that Mary deserved to be scolded for not helping out in the kitchen.

We all have our strengths, our own personal traits. Martha's strength was to serve. There are some people that are good at hospitality. They will make sure their guests have everything that they need. Some people simply have eyes to serve. They realize after a church potluck that tables and chairs need to be taken down. While others just get up and go home. Some get up and wash dishes while others sit and talk. Some people just have a heart to serve. But do we serve with the wrong attitude? When we serve, do we point our finger at someone else, just like Martha did? "Look at me Lord, I am teaching Sunday School, helping with children's church, helping with Bible School, I'm cooking meals for those who are sick—I'm doing all of this and so in so is over there hardly doing anything. Why am I working myself to death while they do nothing?" That is the Martha attitude.

There was no doubt in Martha's mind that her work was extremely important and that Mary deserved to be scolded for not helping out in the kitchen.

You need to do what you are called to do, but don't get frustrated looking at others and seeing what they are not doing. Maybe God has not called them to be a Sunday school teacher. It could be that the other person needs to mature more in their faith before God calls them to do what you are doing. If you have a strong walk with the Lord, you are going to have a passion to serve. You will be looking for ways to serve the Lord. I don't care if I'm the only one in the church serving—I have to do it. My love for God compels me to do His work. I am called to use my time & talents for the Lord. Stop focusing on how other people are serving or are not serving—just do what the Lord has called *you* to do.

Sometimes doing what the Lord has called you to do will require a sacrifice. After Jesus' resurrection, Peter got caught up in comparing his service to others. Jesus tells Peter in John 21:18, *"I tell you the truth, when you were younger you dressed yourself and went where you wanted; but when you are old you will stretch out your hands, and someone else will dress you and lead you where you do not want to go."* Jesus was telling Peter that he was going to die for his faith. What was Peter's reaction? "What about him?" He was speaking of another disciple. What is he going to have to sacrifice? Jesus basically said, "Don't worry about him, just do what I've called you to do." Peter was going to lose his life in service to Jesus. The apostle John was going to live to be an old man. Peter's concern was not supposed to be John's calling, it was supposed to be his own calling. It would be nice if 100% of the people in the church did what they were called to do. But unfortunately a handful of people do most of the work. It would be very easy to get resentful of someone who has chosen the easier path. But my accountability is to God; to do what He asks. My focus should be on God when I serve, not on what others are doing. Martha felt abandoned in her serving-left alone. Maybe there are others who feel the same way. "I have this heavy burden upon me, and no one wants to help me."

It seems like Martha's hard work and devotion are being belittled. But, it's important to understand that Jesus was grateful for her efforts. Jesus was a traveling preacher, going from town to town. He must have appreciated being invited to someone's home to rest and to have a great home cooked meal. And if Martha wouldn't have opened up her home and served Jesus…Mary wouldn't have been able to sit at Jesus' feet. Martha's self-sacrifice allowed Mary to experience Jesus. It is the same way in the church. There are many people who put in a lot of effort so there can be a Bible believing worship service in their local community…so that others can come and sit at Jesus' feet and soak in His teaching and His presence. If it wasn't for the hard work of so many people, we would have dying churches that don't feed anyone spiritually. No one would want to sit at Jesus' feet in a church where there is no Martha. Fortunately, we have people in our churches who love to serve the Lord. I don't think Jesus is rebuking Martha for her service, but rather for her attitude. I will talk a little more about her attitude in a little while, but what a beautiful thing Martha was doing for Jesus. What a beautiful thing you are doing for Jesus as you serve!

> *It would be very easy to get resentful of someone who has chosen the easier path. But my accountability is to God, to do what He asks.*

Mary's Worshipful Attitude

It is interesting to look at Mary's life. Every time Mary (the sister of Martha) is mentioned in the Bible, we see her at Jesus' feet. In John 11, when her brother Lazarus died, Jesus came into town and Mary ran out to meet Him and fell at His feet. In John 12, we find Martha serving another meal. Mary fell before Jesus and took a jar of perfume and put it on Jesus' feet and wiped it with her hair. And in this passage, we see her just sitting at Jesus' feet, listening to whatever He was saying. Mary treasured the time that she was able to spend with Jesus. She soaked up every moment with the Lord. She received joy by just being with Him.

We need to get to the place in our lives where we are like Mary; enjoying Jesus' presence. Most Christians find no joy in reading God's Word or spending time with Him in prayer. They believe that God's Word is boring, and that they have better things to do. Christians need to develop a love for the Word of God. In Psalm 119:103 the psalmist says, *"How sweet are your words to my taste, sweeter than honey to my mouth!"* The psalmist treasured God's Word—and we take it for granted. In Asia, they desire to read God's Word, but they aren't able to get it. There was a church that had only one Bible for the entire church. They ripped it apart and gave 20 pages to each person. The congregation would go home and read it, and bring it back and exchange it for another 20 pages. The Bible is the life giving, life changing Word of God, and we are too busy to read it. We believe that we have other things that are more important than sitting at the feet of Jesus and learning from Him.

Martha's problem surfaced because she was worried and distracted about many things. No one should ever be too busy, or pressured, or too tired to make time for God. After all, God has to manage the whole world, and He's never too busy for us. Our lives are so busy and so stressful that sometimes

> *Mary treasured the time that she was able to spend with Jesus. She soaked up every moment with the Lord.*

we don't think we have time to sit at Jesus' feet. Obviously Martha didn't think she had time to pause and sit before the Lord; she had a meal to make. Martin Luther, a great church reformer once said, "Today is going to be a busy day, I better spend another hour in prayer." That is the attitude Mary had. Is that our attitude? Today is going to be a tough day with lots of challenges in it…today is going to be busy with little time to spare…I better pray another hour. Usually it is the opposite. We don't have time to pray so we say a two minute prayer and out the door we go. But things seem to go much smoother when we spend time with the Lord. It is during that time that we get the strength to serve. It is during that time that God gives us answers for the problems we will face that day. It could be a way that helps us to become more focused upon God, allowing us to start our day off with the right attitude. Taking time with God is inviting Him to *go ahead* of you during your day which allows Him to prepare the way for you. Many people feel like they are losing time out of their day when they pray. The reality is that they are gaining strength and wisdom for the day which makes their day more productive.

I want you to see that neither Martha nor Mary did anything wrong. Jesus did not lecture Martha about how poor her service was. He was just saying that Mary had chosen what was <u>better</u>. We need to make sure we don't sacrifice being fed spiritually so that we can serve more. Some may say, "I don't read the Bible because I use that time to serve others." No, we need to spend time at the feet of Jesus by digging into His Word, praying, memorizing scripture, and simply having fellowship with Him, so that we can be filled up with His strength to serve others.

There will be times, if we are not spending quality time with the Lord, that we will get frustrated in our service. Things won't work out like we planned, and people won't help us like we think they should. So we will get frustrated and quit, like Martha, and even maybe have a bad attitude in our service to the Lord.

If you are serving the Lord in a certain position and you find yourself repeatedly frustrated and harboring bad attitudes…get out. The Lord doesn't want you to serve Him if you are irritable and taking it out on others.

> *Martin Luther, a great church reformer once said, "Today is going to be a busy day, I better spend another hour in prayer."*

Don't serve the Lord in that capacity. Find a way to serve the Lord in which you can be a good example. Mary sitting at Jesus' feet shouldn't have affected Martha's attitude in service. No one should affect your attitude as you serve the Lord. You are serving God to show Him your devotion. If people don't help you, and you have to do more—you are giving more of a sacrifice of love to Him. Instead of getting frustrated, praise God that you can serve Him in a greater way.

Jesus modeled to us the importance of spending time with our heavenly Father. Mark 1:35 says, *"Very early in the morning, while it was still dark, Jesus got up, left the house and went off to a solitary place, where he prayed."* Jesus must have thought it was important to pray because He got up while it was still dark—it was early in the morning. If you read the passage just before this verse, you will see that Jesus had a late night of ministry. He was up late healing the people who came to Him. Yet He went to pray to His Father very early in the morning. He knew the time that He had with His Father would help Him in His ministry. There were times, if Jesus wasn't connected to the Father, that He could have become frustrated or mad and quit serving. He could have decided not to serve God when there were people who were out to kill Him. Yet Jesus, so connected to the Father, served Him even when it took Him to the cross.

Jesus did things that were beneath someone of His stature. Even though He was God, and He created the entire world, He got down and washed the disciple's feet. He washed the disciple's feet with a good attitude and He taught us to do the same. Spending time with God helps us serve the Lord with a good attitude.

I guarantee that if we are open to the Lord's calling in our lives that He will call us to do something that we don't necessarily want to do. Will we quit? Will we cry and complain while we serve like Martha did? Or will we serve the Lord with a smile on our face and with love in our hearts? Our joy in serving, and in the Christian life, comes from taking the time to sit at His feet.

CHAPTER 6

Temptations We Face

I once learned about one way that Eskimos kill a wolf. The first thing the Eskimo does is coat his knife blade with animal blood. He then allows it to freeze. Then he adds another layer of blood, then another layer of blood, until the blade is completely concealed by frozen blood. Next the Eskimo buries his knife in the ground with the blade facing up. When a wolf follows his sensitive nose to the source of the scent and discovers the bait, he licks it, tasting the fresh frozen blood. He begins to lick it faster, more and more vigorously, lapping the blade until the edge is bare. In the cold Arctic night, the wolf licks the blade harder and harder. So great becomes the craving for blood that the wolf does not notice the razor sharp sting of the naked blade on his own tongue nor does he recognize the instant at which his thirst for blood is being quenched by his own blood. He actually is thrilled because the blood is more and more plentiful. His carnivorous appetite just craves more—until the dawn finds him dead in the snow! This gives us fresh insight into the self-destructive nature of sin. We want something bad enough that we don't see the cost. Satan lures us to the place where he plans to ravage us with some sort of destructive fleshly pleasure such as gossip, rage, or sexual sin. Once we give into its lustful pleasures, our cravings for it increases. When we continue to allow ourselves to indulge it grips us even more. And before we know it...it completely consumes us. Satan has come to steal, kill and destroy. Satan's bait is always intended to harm you.[8]

Satan's temptations will draw us away from God's plan for our lives. We start doing something that seems pleasurable, but we soon find out that it brings death to our spiritual being. In Luke 4, we read that Satan even tempts Jesus to turn away from God's plan, and follow His own path in life.

> [1] *Jesus, full of the Holy Spirit, returned from the Jordan and was led by the Spirit in the desert,* [2] *where for forty days he was tempted by the devil. He ate nothing during those days, and at the end of them he was hungry.*
>
> [3] *The devil said to him, "If you are the Son of God, tell this stone to become bread."*
>
> [4] *Jesus answered, "It is written: 'Man does not live on bread alone.'"*
>
> [5] *The devil led him up to a high place and showed him in an instant all the kingdoms of the world.* [6] *And he said to him, "I will give you all their authority and splendor, for it has been given to me, and I can give it to anyone I want to.* [7] *So if you worship me, it will all*

be yours."

⁸ Jesus answered, "It is written: 'Worship the Lord your God and serve him only.'"

⁹ The devil led him to Jerusalem and had him stand on the highest point of the temple. "If you are the Son of God," he said, "throw yourself down from here. ¹⁰ For it is written:

"'He will command his angels concerning you to guard you carefully;

¹¹ they will lift you up in their hands, so that you will not strike your foot against a stone.'"

¹² Jesus answered, "It says: 'Do not put the Lord your God to the test.'"

¹³ When the devil had finished all this tempting, he left him until an opportune time.

As we study the temptations of Jesus, we see the ways in which Satan likes to tempt us. We also learn that the temptations of Jesus are all orchestrated by God. In Verse 1 it says, *"Jesus, full of the Holy Spirit, returned from the Jordan and was <u>led</u> by the Spirit in the desert."* God led Him into the desert to allow Satan to tempt Him. He was being tested by God and being tempted by Satan. It was the very beginning of His ministry and this was a great test to see what kind of Messiah He was going to be. It was time to find out if He would fall into the same traps that mankind has been falling into since the beginning of time. As we go through these temptations, you will see that Jesus quotes the book of Deuteronomy three times. These verses help us to better understand the temptations of Jesus. When Israel was wandering around in the wilderness for 40 years, they were tempted in the same ways as Jesus, and they failed the tests. Deuteronomy 8:2 says, *"Remember how the Lord your God led you all the way in the desert these forty years, to humble you and to test you in order to know what was in your heart, whether or not you would keep his commands."* God tested the Israelites for 40 years to see what was in their hearts, and to find out if they would rely on Him. Then Jesus was in the wilderness for 40 days, and Satan went after Him as well.

Temptation Of Being Self Sufficient

The first temptation was to persuade Jesus to believe He didn't need to look to the Father for His needs; to persuade Jesus to believe that He could provide for Himself with His own power. Verse 1 tells us that Jesus was led into the wilderness by the Holy Spirit. Jesus knew that if the Father would lead Him to a specific place, then the Father would also provide for Him. It wasn't up to Him to take things into His own hands. Consider how tempting this would be for Jesus. He had been in the desert for 40 days without anything to eat. Satan didn't tempt Jesus after a feast in Nazareth. The devil is no dummy. He knows the best time to attack. He waited until Jesus' hunger was the greatest and His resistance would be the lowest. Can you imagine how tempting it would be for Jesus to give in and assume that the Father would want Him to eat? Most of us, if we had the power, would turn stones into bread if we skipped one meal.

What would we do after waiting 40 days?

This was a big test at the outset of Jesus' ministry. Was He completely relying on the Father in tough situations, or would He step up and take matters into His own hands?

> **Jesus knows that if the Father would lead Him to the place that He is, the Father will also provide for Him. It wasn't up to Him to take things into His own hands.**

Jesus responds to Satan's temptation in verse 4, *"Jesus answered, 'It is written: 'Man does not live on bread alone.'"* Jesus is quoting a portion of scripture here. It is an Old Testament passage to show that Israel failed this test when God gave it to them. They found it hard to wait upon God to give them the provisions for their lives. The verse He quotes is Deuteronomy 8:3, which says, *"He humbled you, causing you to hunger and then feeding you with manna, which neither you nor your fathers had known, to teach you that man does not live on bread alone but on every word that comes from the mouth of the Lord."* Do you remember the story of the Israelites and the manna? God gave them specific instructions about how He was going to provide for them. God was going to send down manna every morning except for the Sabbath morning. Each morning they were supposed to gather only enough for that day. The only exception was on the days before the Sabbath, when they were supposed to gather twice as much. The extra portion was to be saved and eaten on the Sabbath. The Israelites acted with their stomachs and ignored what God told them. The first day they collected much more than they could eat, saving some of it for the next day. I am sure they were thinking, "Who knows if there will be manna given to us tomorrow? We had better collect it while it is here." But when they woke up the next day, there were maggots all over the manna. Then, as the Sabbath drew near, they were supposed to collect twice the amount on the sixth day, because none was given on the Sabbath. Yet they went out on the Sabbath and tried to find manna to eat. They found it hard to rely on God for their provisions.

God wasn't pleased with Israel. Jesus knew better and came to show us the right way. Do we trust the Lord to provide our daily bread? In the Lord's Prayer, Jesus teaches us to pray, "Give us this day our daily bread." It doesn't say to give us a month's worth, so that we don't have to be dependent on Him each day. Do we see the food we eat every day as God providing richly for us? Proverbs 30:8-9 says, *"Keep falsehood and lies far from me; give me neither poverty nor riches, but give me only my daily bread. Otherwise, I may have too much and disown you and say, 'Who is the Lord?' Or I may become poor and steal, and so dishonor the name of my God."* Sometimes we work harder and harder, not to provide for our daily needs, but to store up more. We too often try to become self sufficient. We wouldn't say it, but sometimes, the way we live our lives is our way of saying, "I can make it without God. Why do I need the Bible to teach me how to live, I'm doing pretty good on my own."

> *In the Lord's Prayer, Jesus teaches us to pray, "Give us this day our daily bread." It doesn't say to give us a month's worth, so that we don't have to be dependent on Him each day.*

The Temptation Of Taking The Easy Way Out

Oh how tempting this second temptation might have been for Jesus. Satan says, "Worship me and I will give you all the kingdoms of the world." Satan has the power to do that. The Bible says on many occasions that he is the prince of this world, and the ruler of the kingdom of the air. God has given Satan authority to rule for a time on this earth. And Satan said he would share his power with Jesus if Jesus would worship him. Jesus knew that one day He would rule the earth—that was already part of God's plan, but Satan was offering Him a way to rule the earth without going to the cross. Satan was offering a kingdom and all its glory without the suffering. Satan was tempting Jesus to believe that he could provide a better way for Him than God could. Satan's logic was, "After all, with God's way you have to suffer; I'm not asking you to suffer. It's all yours. All you have to do is worship me." What an amazing deal!! Most people would, and do, jump on the deals that Satan offers them. It is the easy way.

But can you see the catch in what Satan was offering Jesus? It is the same catch in anything that he offers us as well. What he offers is only temporary. God's way—Jesus is going to be King of Kings for all eternity. Satan's way—Jesus would have authority for a time, until Satan no longer has control of this world. Jesus responds to this temptation by quoting a portion of Deuteronomy 6:13, *"Fear the Lord your God, serve him only and take your oaths in his name."* The Israelites failed at worshipping only God. When they were in the desert, they built a golden calf and they started to worship it. They were distracted from worshipping God for a temporary pleasure of serving the god of gold they made with their hands.

> *Satan was offering a kingdom and all its glory without the suffering. Satan was tempting Jesus to believe that he could provide a better way for Him than God could.*

How often have we chosen the easy way out because we want our pleasures met immediately and we don't want to deny ourselves? We serve the god of this world; the money and the earthly possessions. We must see that Satan's way is attractive to us because there seems to be no cost…but if we follow his plan we will lose everything in the end. When we take the easy road in life, and avoid the cross, we are worshipping something we shouldn't. We will reap temporary rewards. But while God's way may bring sacrifices, it yields an eternal reward. Would you prefer five dollars now or a million dollars next week? Do you desire the sinful pleasures now, or eternal life in heaven?

The Temptation To Test God And Force His Hand

Satan takes Jesus to the highest point of the temple and tells Him, "If you are the Son of God, jump down and God will rescue you." Prove to me that you are the Son of God. Jesus faced this temptation more than once. While He was on the cross, people cried out, "Come down off that cross and we will believe that you are the Christ." Prove it to us. Jesus could have come down off the cross and they would have known without a doubt that He was the Christ, but they still would have been lost in their sins. Jesus had to stay on the cross and die. When Satan tempted Jesus to jump off the temple, Jesus could have easily jumped and proved that He was the Christ, but He would have been forcing God's hand. He would have been making the Father come through for Him, instead of Him doing what the Father wanted Him to do.

Jesus basically said, "I will trust my Father to do things His way, not mine." Jesus quotes a portion of Deuteronomy 6:16, that says, *"Do not test the Lord your God as you did at Massah."* To better understand His response, we have to go to Exodus 17. Exodus 17:5-7 says, *"The Lord answered Moses, 'Walk on ahead of the people. Take with you some of the elders of Israel and take in your hand the staff with which you struck the Nile, and go. I will stand there before you by the rock at Horeb. Strike the rock, and water will come out of it for the people to drink.' So Moses did this in the sight of the elders of Israel. And he called the place Massah and Meribah because the Israelites quarreled and because they tested the Lord saying, 'Is the Lord among us or not?'"* Massah means testing. The people were crying out in the desert because they were thirsty. They wanted the Lord to prove He was there by giving them water. People always want God to prove Himself.

Sometimes we want God to serve us, instead of us serving Him. We believe that when we do things like starting a new ministry, that surely God will come right to our aid and bless it. Or we might believe that if we go out and spend all of the money we have to live on this week, then surely God is a faithful God, and He will provide for our every need. We live our lives by our own way, and we expect God to be faithful to come and catch us. We need to seek God and ask Him what He wants us to do. We need to find out what God is doing around us and join Him in His work. Seek God on how to spend your money, don't spend it all and expect Him to bail you out. Don't put God to the test. Serve Him; don't expect Him to serve you.

The Weapons We Have To Fight Temptation

Jesus' temptations were real, not merely symbolic. Hebrews 4:15 says, *"For we do not have a high priest who is unable to sympathize with our weaknesses, but we have one who has been tempted in every way, just as we are—yet was without sin."* He was confronted by Satan with a real opportunity to sin and have an easier life for Himself. But Jesus stuck to the will of His Father in heaven and never gave in to temptation.

There were a couple of things in this Luke 4 passage that helped Jesus resist the temptations. One was the Holy Spirit. Verse 1 starts out saying, *"Jesus, full of the Holy Spirit."* Often Satan finds little resistance when he comes to tempt us because we have more of the world

> *Jesus' temptations were real, not merely symbolic...He was confronted by Satan with a real opportunity to sin and have an easier life for Himself.*

in us than we do of God's Spirit. We need to be full of the Holy Spirit. Ephesians 5:18 says, *"Do not get drunk on wine, which leads to debauchery. Instead, be filled with the Spirit."* Don't gratify the lusts of the flesh, be filled with the Spirit. The Greek word "filled" here is not a one-time experience. We are filled with the Spirit when we accept Jesus as our Savior. But this verse "filled" is in the present tense, which shows us that we need to be repeatedly filled with the Spirit.

I would like to give you an image to think about. It speaks to us and our continual need to be filled with the Holy Spirit. The great preacher D.L. Moody said, "The easiest way to keep a broken vessel full is to keep the faucet constantly running."[9] Can you picture a broken vessel under a faucet? If you take it away from the faucet the water will leak out of it. But if it is kept under the flow of the water, it will always be full. We are broken vessels; broken by sin. If we try to follow Christ once in a while, we are going to be empty vessels. But if we are continually reading the Bible, praying, and meditating on His Word, we will be continually filled by the Holy Spirit.

If your soul is not quenched by the Spirit of God, you will go looking for something in the world to quench your longings. We were created to worship. If we are not worshipping God, we will find something else to worship. We can't resist the devil if we are trying to do it on our own power; we need God's help.

The second thing that helped Jesus resist temptation was that He had the Word of God memorized. When He was tempted to sin, He quoted the Bible to Satan. When we know the Word of God, and it lives in us…our lives display the character of God. Ephesians 6 provides details about the armor of God. We are told that the Word of God is our only offensive weapon in the fight against Satan. We need to know it well. We can't be satisfied with having God's Word in the back of our minds from when we attended Sunday school 20 years ago. The Word of God needs to be actively moving in our thoughts, so we can speak it to Satan when he tries to persuade us to compromise.

Satan was desperately trying to cause Jesus to sin because he knew if he could bring Jesus down, it would bring everyone of us down with Him. But Jesus remained submissive to the Father's plan. And now Satan knows he is defeated! Jesus conquered sin, and He conquered death.

> *The Word of God needs to be actively moving in our thoughts, so we can speak it to Satan when he tries to persuade us to compromise.*

Satan knows his time is short, so now he is coming to try to defeat each one of us. Are you falling for Satan's temptations? Do you believe that he has an easier life for you, one that is more independent from God, and one that will not cost you much? We need to respond to Satan in the same way that Jesus did. We need to listen to God's Word, not our own words. We need to understand that Satan is just trying to trick us and bring us down. But we also need to realize that God cares for us and will lead us in the right direction. Don't be like the wolf in the opening story of this chapter and allow yourself to be tempted by the bait of Satan. Submit yourself to God's Word and Spirit, and reap the eternal rewards.

CHAPTER 7

Listening To The Wrong Voice

There was a lunch party at an office one day. It was a warm, Chicago day in early September, and the windows were wide open. Soon a bee found its way in, and after buzzing around us for a while it landed on some food on the table. One of the women at the table took an empty bottle of sparkling grape juice and put the mouth of the bottle near the bee. When she did that, everyone expected the bee to be startled and fly away for its own safety. Instead, without a moment's hesitation, the bee flew to the mouth of the bottle and climbed inside the narrow opening. Immediately she put the cap on the bottle and screwed it shut. What was the lady's purpose in luring the bee into the bottle? Was she concerned about the bee, wanting it to enjoy our hospitality and have plenty to drink? No, she disliked the bee. Her purpose was to capture and control. The bee had flown into a trap. When Satan incites us to indulge in the pleasures of the world in a manner that oversteps God's commands, what is his purpose? Is he concerned that we might miss out on some good things in life? No, he despises humans. His purpose is to capture and control. We must never forget that when we follow Satan, we walk into his trap.[10]

We need to make sure we are not walking into Satan's trap. God tells us in John 10, that we need to follow Him and be mindful not to stray from His fold.

> [1] *"I tell you the truth, the man who does not enter the sheep pen by the gate, but climbs in by some other way, is a thief and a robber.* [2] *The man who enters by the gate is the shepherd of his sheep.* [3] *The watchman opens the gate for him, and the sheep listen to his voice. He calls his own sheep by name and leads them out.* [4] *When he has brought out all his own, he goes on ahead of them, and his sheep follow him because they know his voice.* [5] *But they will never follow a stranger; in fact, they will run away from him because they do not recognize a stranger's voice."* [6] *Jesus used this figure of speech, but they did not understand what he was telling them.*
>
> [7] *Therefore Jesus said again, "I tell you the truth, I am the gate for the sheep.* [8] *All who ever came before me were thieves and robbers, but the sheep did not listen to them.* [9] *I am the gate; whoever enters through me will be saved. He will come in and go out, and find pasture.* [10] *The thief comes only to steal and kill and destroy; I have come that they may have life, and have it to the full.*
>
> [11] *"I am the good shepherd. The good*

shepherd lays down his life for the sheep. [12] *The hired hand is not the shepherd who owns the sheep. So when he sees the wolf coming, he abandons the sheep and runs away. Then the wolf attacks the flock and scatters it.* [13] *The man runs away because he is a hired hand and cares nothing for the sheep.*

[14] *"I am the good shepherd; I know my sheep and my sheep know me—* [15] *just as the Father knows me and I know the Father—and I lay down my life for the sheep.* [16] *I have other sheep that are not of this sheep pen. I must bring them also. They too will listen to my voice, and there shall be one flock and one shepherd.* [17] *The reason my Father loves me is that I lay down my life—only to take it up again.* [18] *No one takes it from me, but I lay it down of my own accord. I have authority to lay it down and authority to take it up again. This command I received from my Father."*

Whose Voice Are You Listening To?

There are two voices in this passage who are trying to get the sheep's attention. The sheep respond to the voice that they are familiar with, and they stay clear of the voice they don't recognize. There are people who call me on the phone and they do not tell me who they are; they just start talking. I can tell who some of them are by the sound of their voice. When my wife Janelle calls me, she doesn't need to say, "Hey Kurt, this is Janelle." She just starts talking and I recognize her voice right away. I recognize her voice because I am in a covenant relationship with her and I have had many conversations with her. There are other people who just start talking to me, and it takes me a while to figure out who it is. I keep talking awhile trying to get some clues that will help me figure out who I am actually talking to. But sometimes I have to end up asking, "Who is this I am talking to?" I haven't had many experiences with these people and have not heard their voice enough to discern who it is.

In verse 3, Jesus says, *"The watchman opens the gate for him, and the sheep listen to his voice. He calls his own sheep by name and leads them out."* The sheep know the shepherds voice. When the shepherd watched over his sheep, he would talk and sing so the sheep could be comforted by his voice. The sheep heard the voice of their shepherd and they knew they were safe. There was no mistaking his voice because they heard it so often.

In the same way, God is our shepherd and we need to know His voice. When we read the Bible, pray, and spend time in church, we know His voice so well that we know when God is speaking to us. Much like I know Janelle's voice because we are in

> **The sheep heard the voice of their shepherd and they knew they were safe. There was no mistaking his voice because they heard it so often.**

a close covenant relationship with one another, so I know God's voice when He speaks to me because I am in a close covenant relationship with Him. I have had many different experiences with Him. Those sheep who are truly in a covenant relationship with Him will recognize His voice. If they aren't in a covenant relationship with Jesus, they are likely listening to the world's voices too much to be able to discern God's voice.

Verse 5 continues to talk about the sheep, *"But they will never follow a stranger; in fact, they will run away from him because they do not recognize a stranger's voice."* Sheep are frightened very easily. Sheep are scared of strangers. They want to hear the shepherd's voice. If a stranger tries to tempt the sheep with green grass, the sheep will run away because they don't recognize his voice. It doesn't matter that he has green grass; he is not the shepherd. That is how we should react to Satan's voice. We should run from Satan's voice when he tries to get us to do things that will draw us away from the flock.

Verse 4 says, *"When he has brought out all his own, he goes on ahead of them, and his sheep follow him because they know his voice."* Sheep are different than cattle. In the movies, you see cowboys herding cattle. They get behind them and they yell and holler to get the cows to go in a certain direction. But sheep are not driven from behind like cattle. With sheep, the shepherd goes ahead of them and just speaks or sings, and the sheep listen to his voice. The sheep want to follow the shepherd because the shepherd always leads them to places that are good for them.

In the same way, Jesus goes ahead of us in our lives and He speaks to us. We should want to follow Him because we know He will always lead us to places that are good for us. God is not going to get behind us and drive us to go a certain direction. God will not force you to go where you do not want to go. He will lead and let you choose whether or not you will follow. Are you open to listening to His voice and to go where He leads you?

There was a man working late one night in his office. He was the only one in the building and he was up on the 6th floor. As he shut off his computer and made his way to the elevator, he began to see smoke in the hall way. He knew he couldn't take the elevator down, so he headed for the stairs. When he got to the stairs, he saw there was smoke coming up from the stairwell. He wasn't sure what to do, so he ran back to his office and opened the window. He saw the fire department was down there and they told him to get out on the ledge and jump—into the net that was set up to catch him. The man got out on the ledge, and looked down, he could not see the net because there was too much smoke along the edge of the building. He couldn't get himself to jump because he couldn't see the net. The fire chief was on the blow horn reassuring him that he would be ok, and that there was a net below to catch him. But no matter what the fire chief said, the man couldn't bring himself to jump. He couldn't see the net. Then a familiar voice, his father, got on and said. "Son, it is ok. You can jump. There is a net that will catch you." It was that familiar voice, that voice he could trust, the voice he knew wanted what was best for him—that gave the man the courage to jump even though he couldn't see where he would land."[11]

God is not going to make you follow. He is not going to make you jump. It is your choice. But if you are in this covenant relationship with Him, you are going to want to follow where He leads because His words are life and peace to you. You wouldn't want to be anywhere else than within His care.

But God is not going to get behind us and drive us to go a certain direction. God will not force you to go where you do not want to go.

Are You Really Protected?

In verses 11-13, Jesus says, *"I am the good shepherd. The good shepherd lays down his life for the sheep. The hired hand is not the shepherd who owns the sheep. So when he sees the wolf coming, he abandons the sheep and runs away. Then the wolf attacks the flock and scatters it. The man runs away because he is a hired hand and cares nothing for the sheep."* There are two different people watching over the sheep in this passage. One is doing it out of love and the other is doing it for his own self interests. The hired hand is only watching the sheep to get a paycheck. According to the law, they were not responsible for wild animals that would come and attack the flock. Exodus 22:13 tells us that the hired hand is not liable. *"If it was torn to pieces by a wild animal, he shall bring in the remains as evidence and he will not be required to pay for the torn animal."* It is clear that a hired hand has no investment in whether or not the sheep are safe from wild animals. So if a wild animal comes, he is going to leave the sheep to fend for itself—he is going to protect himself.

    Jesus was obviously telling the Pharisees that they were the hired hands in these verses. The Pharisees cared nothing for the sheep, they cared nothing about the people they were leading. They were the spiritual leaders, but they didn't love their followers. They led the people because it benefited them financially, and because it gave them a good name and a good reputation. They would have never thought about going out of their way to protect their sheep from harm. If it wasn't going to benefit them, they would leave their sheep to fend for themselves. It is sad to see the same thing happening today. There are many false teachers leading the sheep of God, pastors that only care about themselves and their reputation. They only care about getting a large amount of people following them and about benefiting from those people financially. They don't care what truly happens to their sheep; they are only in it for themselves. False teachers will tell you whatever you want to hear to keep you happy; to keep you coming to church; to keep you giving or serving in the church. "You're ok. You can continue to live that way." Look at Jeremiah 6:14. God was talking about the false teachers. *"They dress the wound of my people as though it were not serious. 'Peace, peace,' they say, when there is no peace."* In this passage, God was frustrated at false teachers telling the people that everything is ok. All the while, God was ready to send the people into exile for their rebellion against Him. The people were on the path to destruction; exile was coming and these teachers are holding Israel's hands on the path to exile away from God. If only these teachers would have shared the truth! It was not what the people wanted to hear, but it would have given them a chance to repent and steer clear of the destruction that was to come.

We see the exact same thing happening today. Preachers and church goers are telling people, "You are alright. What you are doing is fine." All the while, God is saying, "You are living in rebellion against me." These false teachers don't really care about protecting you. If they did they would be concerned about driving the evil away from you. Most people don't want to hurt you with the truth, they would rather be your friend and let you live a lie. Be careful that you are not following a hired hand that cares nothing for your spiritual well being—someone who is only concerned with flattering you and keeping you happy by saying whatever you want to hear. Surround yourself with people who will speak the truth in love, even if it is something you don't want to hear.

The second person watching over the sheep is the good shepherd. The good shepherd is totally different than the hired hand. He is not only there to lead you to the green pastures to eat and the quiet waters to drink; the hired hand does that, too. But what sets the good shepherd apart from the hired hand is in John 10:11. *"I am the good shepherd. The good shepherd lays down his life for the sheep."* When the wild animal comes, the shepherd runs toward the danger to help the sheep fight it off. He cares for the sheep and he does not want the wolf to devour it. If he has to die to protect the sheep from the evil, he is more than willing. Jesus boldly says, *"I am the good shepherd and I lay down my life for my sheep."* That is what Jesus was willing to do. Jesus saw the enemy, the devil, coming to devour us. He could have left us to defend for ourselves, but He cares too much for us. So He came to earth and laid down His life on the cross to protect us. Jesus died on the cross to defeat Satan once and for all.

If we live in His flock, under his protective hand, Satan cannot devour us. But if we choose to stray, Satan will be right there to pounce on us. In verse 10, Jesus says, *"The thief comes only to steal and kill and destroy; I have come that they may have life, and have it to the full."* Satan comes to steal and kill and destroy. Just like the opening story with the bee and the bottle—Satan sets out the trap, not to bless you with something good, but to harm you and to destroy you. He wants to bring you to financial ruin. He wants to ruin your marriage, bring strife in your family, and keep you from coming to church. He wants to bring conflict into your life in any way that he can, and keep you focused on yourself and on the things of this world! Satan will gladly have fresh grass in his hands to lure the sheep away from the fold. But once that grass is gone, he has no plans to give the sheep more grass. He uses that grass to destroy them.

We would not follow him if he told us that he was coming to kill and destroy us. So he tempts us with "financial gain" which leads us to cheating, or to a heart of greed for more things of the world. Or he tempts us with a "relationship" that will draw us away from God's will for our lives; he tempts us with "popularity" only to get us to strive more for the attention of man instead of the attention of God. How is Satan tempting you with a hand full of grass? He doesn't have any more grass for you! Don't follow him!

It is easy to see the difference between Jesus and Satan. Satan wants to kill and destroy you. Jesus was willing to lay down His life to give you eternal life with Him.

Satan will gladly have fresh grass in his hands to lure the sheep away from the fold. But once that grass is gone, he has no plans to give the sheep more grass.

His voice is calling out to us today. In verse 16, Jesus says, *"I have other sheep that are not of this sheep pen. I must bring them also. They too will listen to my voice, and there shall be one flock and one shepherd."* Jesus was telling the Jews that there are more sheep out in the world that will listen to His voice. He was telling them that He was going to call the Gentiles to follow Him as well. It was unheard of that a Gentile could be a follower of God, but Jesus was now opening it up to those who appeared not to be deserving of it. Maybe there are people reading this that are not from a religious upbringing. You may be wondering why Jesus would want you, considering the life you have lived. Jesus is calling out to you today, "You can come and be a part of my flock. All you have to do is hear my voice and follow me."

Jesus also says in verse 7, *"I tell you the truth, I am the gate for the sheep."* A fence would provide shelter from the wild animals and keep the sheep safe. <u>The gate</u> was the only way into that protection. Jesus says, "I am the gate…I am the only way in." He says something similar in John 14:6, *"Jesus answered, 'I am the way, and the truth, and the life. No one comes to the Father except through me.'"* Jesus is the only way to salvation. All other roads lead you outside of heaven. All other roads lead to being devoured by the enemy.

I don't know what is happening in your individual life today. There are probably 100 different things going on in each of your lives right now. But please make sure you are entering through the gate, which is the narrow way to the protection Jesus provides…and not being lured away by the other voices of the world. Do things Jesus' way, even when you don't understand why. Be willing to follow His voice just because you know His voice will <u>always</u> lead you on the right path.

CHAPTER 8

Caught Up In Spiritual Warfare

I love to play baseball, and I played as a small little tike all the way through college. But there is one game in particular that I will never forget. Our team was up to bat and the pitcher threw the ball in the dirt, and the catcher got in front of it—but it bounced off of him towards our dug out. He came running after it, and all of a sudden when he was right in front of our bench, he fell to the ground. It hit him where he was not protected. The catcher for their team didn't wear certain protection that a man should wear…a cup! I will always remember that and wonder why he wouldn't wear the protection that he needed?

As a catcher, you have equipment that you need to wear—you have a face mask, chest protector, shin guards, glove and a cup. As a catcher you need all of those items. I wouldn't even think of going out there and catching if I wasn't wearing every one of those items. Could you imagine a catcher going out with a glove and chest protector, leaving his face and his shins exposed? Even if you are a good catcher and you catch everything that is thrown to you, you still need to wear all the gear. Balls will be thrown in the dirt and hit you, or batters will foul tip the ball and it will come back and hit you. I don't know of a catcher who would go out without all their gear. (Well, I guess I do know *one* catcher who went and played without all of his gear and it didn't work out too well for him). Picture life as a baseball game. Spiritually, we have some gear we need to wear, but not everyone is concerned about putting it all on. When we don't wear all of our gear, we leave ourselves open to getting hurt. No matter how good of a Christian we are, we can't stop the attacks of the devil without the gear God has given us to wear.

As a nation, we spend a lot of time and money trying to protect our country. We build bombs, radars, and night vision goggles. We have both offensive and defensive weapons to protect us from our enemies. Locally we hire police men and security guards. We put up lights around our houses and put locks on our doors to keep us safe from physical danger. We do a lot to protect ourselves physically. The question is; do we protect ourselves from Spiritual attacks? There is such a thing as spiritual warfare, and Satan has it in for you.[12] In Ephesians 6, God tells us what is available to us in this fight against Satan.

> *[10] Finally, be strong in the Lord and in his mighty power. [11] Put on the full armor of God so that you can take your stand against the devil's schemes. [12] For our struggle is not against flesh and blood, but against the rulers, against the authorities, against the powers of this dark*

world and against the spiritual forces of evil in the heavenly realms. [13] Therefore put on the full armor of God, so that when the day of evil comes, you may be able to stand your ground, and after you have done everything, to stand. [14] Stand firm then, with the belt of truth buckled around your waist, with the breastplate of righteousness in place, [15] and with your feet fitted with the readiness that comes from the gospel of peace. [16] In addition to all this, take up the shield of faith, with which you can extinguish all the flaming arrows of the evil one. [17] Take the helmet of salvation and the sword of the Spirit, which is the word of God. [18] And pray in the Spirit on all occasions with all kinds of prayers and requests. With this in mind, be alert and always keep on praying for all the saints.

Be Strong In The Lord

Paul instructed the Ephesians to do a lot of things throughout his letter to them. He ended it by saying, *"Be strong in the Lord and in his mighty power."* In other words, "You can't do everything I told you, and you can't resist the devil on your own power." Paul used this powerful illustration to get his point across. He helped his readers by getting them to picture a soldier in this type of armor protecting their land. The people could identify with this analogy because at this time, Rome was occupying the nation of Israel. The Israelites would have seen Roman soldiers wearing their armor every day. The Roman soldiers were always ready for an enemy to attack them. A Roman soldier would never go out without having their armor on, because they didn't know what would happen during the day. They didn't want to be caught unprepared. Can you imagine if a fight broke out, and a soldier had said, "I need to go home and get my armor; I will be right back." No! He needs to be prepared at all times. Paul's point was that we are all soldiers in God's kingdom, and we need to be ready for battle at all times. Never leave your armor at home.

You do not know when your enemy will attack you. A soldier puts on his armor at the beginning of the day and he is ready throughout the day for the enemies' attack. And that is what Paul tells us to do. Verse 11 says,

> ...*we are all soldiers in God's kingdom, and we need to be ready for battle at all times. Never leave your armor at home.*

"Put on the full armor of God so that you can take your stand against the devil's schemes." If you want to be successful against the devil's attacks, you need to be prepared for them. If he catches you sleeping, you don't stand a chance. We can't wait until the devil attacks, to put on the full armor of God. If we wait until he attacks, we are done with. We can't say to the devil, "Stop attacking me for a second, I need to put on my armor to fight you." There is no way he would wait for you. He will attack you when you are at your weakest.

We need to wake up each morning and not only put

on our clothes, but put on the full armor of God. We need to claim victory before we even start the day. We need to plead the blood of Jesus over our day. We need to start the day with prayer, with His Word, and with praise for our God. We need to put on the armor of God before we do anything else because we know we will need it. We don't know at what time, but Satan will attack us many times every day. If you recognize yourself as a soldier, you would never think of leaving the house without your armor. Remember the disciples in the garden before Jesus' death? Jesus told them to, *"Watch and pray."* Why? *"So they will not fall into temptation."* The disciples ended up running away when Jesus was arrested. They didn't prepare themselves for that moment. They let their guard down. Instead of praying, they were sleeping. Many times, we are also unprepared to meet the devil's attacks, and we fall into temptation. We don't take time to protect ourselves from Satan each and every day.

    I like how verse 11 is phrased, *"Stand against the devil's schemes."* The devil is a schemer. He plots for one reason, to tear you down. He wants nothing more than to wound you and to take you out of the fight. Satan will attack you in every area of your life. There is nothing off limits to him. He will try to catch you off guard, and get you when you are at your weakest. But he will also try to overpower you even when you feel like you are strong. We need to be ready at every moment to resist Satan. He attacks sneakily and unannounced. When a war is being fought, the enemy doesn't tell you how and when he is going to attack. You have to be on your toes; ready for anything. This is especially true for the war we are fighting right now; the war on terror. The terrorist's intentions are to kill us. They don't tell us their plans. Satan is the biggest terrorist of them all, (if you will allow me to use that illustration). Satan has declared war on you today and he will not stop attacking you. Just like the soldiers in Iraq did not have a clue when a roadside bomb would go off, we do not know when Satan will bomb us with a spiritually crippling blow.

We know that Satan will come after us. We just don't know when and how. It could be early in the day when you first get to work and people are standing around gossiping, attempting to get you to join in. Hopefully, you are prepared to resist and say, "No, I won't talk about someone like that."

> *We need to be ready at every moment to resist Satan. He attacks sneakily and unannounced. When a war is being fought, the enemy doesn't tell you how and when he is going to attack. You have to be on your toes; ready for anything.*

Maybe Satan will attack you later in the day, trying to get you to be dishonest in your business dealings. If you don't have your armor on, you might not be thinking about how you can please the Lord, but about how you can earn handfuls of extra money. Or the devil can attack you at night. You may get in a situation where you are alone with a person of the opposite sex, tempting you to cheat on your spouse and your God. I can hear people saying, "What will it hurt to fall into the temptation just this one time?" Satan will attack you many different ways and at any given time. I have seen marriages destroyed, businesses collapse, and friendships wrecked because Satan wanted to cause havoc in people's lives. These people were not strong enough to stop him. They weren't prepared for his attack.

We need to recognize who our struggle is against. We are not struggling against a powerful or smart person. We are struggling against Satan. Verse 12 says, *"For our struggle is not against flesh and blood, but against the rulers, against the authorities, against the powers of this dark world and against the spiritual forces of evil in the heavenly realms."* This passage makes it clear that we are not fighting against any certain person. We are fighting with the evil forces trying to persuade our lives. Evil forces are trying to persuade the other people to fight you. If a doctor is treating a patient, and he looks at the symptoms, the doctor doesn't try to treat the symptoms. He tries to stop the underlying problem that is causing the symptoms for the patient. In the same way, in our conflict with each other, we often deal with the symptoms. What we need to do is address the forces of evil that are the underlying problems. We fight against people and try to outsmart them, all the while Satan is congratulating himself on another success for his kingdom. We need to see who we are really fighting against.

The only way we can fight a powerful enemy like this is with the power that God gives us. Satan is too strong for us on our own. But Satan is no match for God. God can give us victory.

We need to recognize who our struggle is against. We are not struggling against a powerful or smart person. We are struggling against Satan.

The Armor Of God

Verse 13 says, *"Therefore put on the full armor of God, so that when the day of evil comes, you may be able to stand your ground, and after you have done everything, to stand. Stand firm."* Again, put it on before the day of trouble comes. It is not a matter of <u>if</u> the day of evil comes, but <u>when</u> the day of evil comes. Don't wait! We are told to put on the <u>full</u> armor of God. We can't put on one or two pieces; we need every item. If you were going into battle, you would not just take your helmet and sword. You would also take your breastplate and shield. Every piece of armor is important in our battle against Satan. Now I want to look at each of the armor really briefly.

Belt of Truth: A Roman soldier would wear one piece of clothing, like a short dress, that stops above the knees. I've never worn that type of clothing before but I can only imagine that without a belt, their clothing would fly all over the place. It would be hard to fight a battle with a dress flapping in the wind. The belt would also hold the sword in place. Truth should be fastened close to us like a belt keeping everything else in check. Truth guards our life so we don't go wherever the wind blows; wherever the next teaching tries to lead us.

Breastplate of righteousness: The breastplate covers our vital organs. If we would get struck there, our wound would be fatal. One of those vital organs is the heart. Jesus said that whatever comes out of our heart makes the man (or woman) you are (whether good or bad). God gave us this breastplate to protect the righteousness He gave us.

Feet fitted with the readiness that comes from the gospel of peace: Shoes make it possible to go more places and to get there quicker than before. Walking barefoot would slow us down because we have to watch our step. And some places we just couldn't go without shoes. This scripture is telling us that we do have shoes, and that we are to go everywhere, as fast as we can, to proclaim the gospel of peace—the gospel of Jesus Christ.

Shield of faith: I love this image. In Biblical times, armies would light their arrows on fire and shoot them at their enemies. A soldier had his shield to protect him from these arrows. Without the shield, he wouldn't stand a chance against those flaming arrows. Satan throws all kinds of fiery arrows at us. He tries to bombard us with temptation after temptation, but we have the shield of our faith to protect us from his temptations. Make sure you pick up your shield before you leave the house in the morning, because Satan has arrows with your name on them.

Helmet of salvation: A helmet guards and protects your head. The helmet of salvation is the knowledge that we are saved. It also guards the thoughts that come into our lives. One of Satan's greatest tricks is to get us thinking about things we shouldn't. If we think about something long enough, it usually leads to action. 2 Corinthians 10:5

says, *"...we take captive every thought to make it obedient to Christ."* We need to take back control of the thoughts that penetrate our minds. If you are thinking about something that you shouldn't...dismiss it. Quote Bible verses. You have a helmet to protect your head; to protect your mind. Don't let Satan strike a blow to your head.

Sword of the spirit which is the word of God: This is the only offensive weapon that we have. It is the Word of God. When we fight the devil we have to defeat him by using God's Word. The tragedy is that most people do not know God's Word very well. So how can they defeat Satan? The Bible is the only way we can beat Satan. He must retreat when we learn how to use this sword. When we don't know how to use it, Satan will not be scared. Learn how to use this sword, and be a powerful soldier for the Lord.

CHAPTER 9

Thinking The Wrong Thoughts

There was a farmer who was continually optimistic, seldom did he get discouraged or blue. He had a neighbor who was the opposite—grim and gloomy, he faced each new morning with a heavy sigh. The happy, optimistic farmer would see the sun coming up and shout over the roar of the tractor, "Look at the beautiful sun and clear sky!" And with a frown the negative neighbor would reply, "Yeah, it'll probably scorch the crops!" When clouds would gather and much needed rain would start to fall, our positive friend would smile across the fence, "ain't this great, God is giving our corn a drink today!" Again, the same negative response, "Uh huh, but if it doesn't stop before too long it'll flood and wash everything away." One day the optimist decided to put his pessimistic neighbor to the maximum test. He bought the smartest, most expensive bird dog he could find. He trained him to do things no other dog on earth could do; impossible feats that would surely astonish anyone. He invited the pessimist to go duck hunting with him. They sat in the boat and the ducks flew all around them. They both shot and several ducks fell into the water. "Go get 'em" the man ordered his dog. The dog leaped out of the boat, walked on the water, and picked up the birds one by one. "Well, what do you think of that?" The pessimist answered, "The dog can't swim can he?"[13]

What kind of attitude do you have? Do you always see the negative aspects of life and put your focus upon that, or can you see the good in everything? The thoughts that we think certainly dictate our emotions, moods, and actions. If you are weighed down with negative thoughts all of the time, you will be grumpy, depressed, and worn out. You can't help being depressed and grumpy if all you have going in your mind are negative thoughts. If you think about the bad things of life, and worry about all of the bad that might happen to you in the days ahead, it will steal your joy. You will not live in the victory that Jesus died to give you. Let your mind rest easy in the fact that God is in control. In Philippians 4 we see that our mind is the key to winning victories in our lives.

> [4] *Rejoice in the Lord always. I will say it again: Rejoice!* [5] *Let your gentleness be evident to all. The Lord is near.* [6] *Do not be anxious about anything, but in everything, by prayer and petition, with thanksgiving, present your requests to God.* [7] *And the peace of God, which transcends all understanding, will guard your hearts and your minds in Christ Jesus.*
>
> [8] *Finally, brothers, whatever is true, whatever is noble, whatever is right, whatever is pure,*

whatever is lovely, whatever is admirable—if anything is excellent or praiseworthy—think about such things.

Our Minds Are The Key To Winning The Victories

Paul started out by saying that we need to rejoice in the Lord always. We shouldn't wait until things are good in our lives and we feel at peace with our situations. We need to have a continual attitude of praise in our heart. If we can learn to live this verse out, our lives will be completely different.

Paul mentions the key to this battle several times. The key to the battle is in our minds. Verse 6 starts out by saying, *"Do not be anxious about anything."* Paul is telling us to guard our thoughts. Why worry and fret over a future problem that might not ever come? And when problems do come, they are usually not near as bad as we play them out in our minds. As we think about our future problems, we always imagine the worst case scenario. We need to start looking at our future in the best case scenario.

Paul goes on in verse 6 to say, *"but in everything, by prayer and petition, with thanksgiving, present your requests to God."* Why worry ourselves to death about this situation when we can just go to God and hand it over to Him? If we go to Him and give Him our anxious minds, like it says in verse 6, then this passage goes on and says in verse 7 that God will give us His peace that transcends all understanding. That peace will guard our hearts and our minds. It is a peace that will keep our minds from being consumed about the "what if's" of life. What if I lose my job? What if I get sick? What if people don't accept me? Release these negative thoughts. Give them to God and receive the peace that transcends all understanding.

Verse 8 goes on to talk more about our minds, and how they are a key component to winning the battle. *"Finally, brothers, whatever is true, whatever is noble, whatever is right, whatever is pure, whatever is lovely, whatever is admirable—if anything is excellent or praise worthy—think about such things."* Think about the things that are excellent and praiseworthy. Think about the things that will build you up. Digging into God's Word daily reminds us that we

> **As we think about our future problems we always imagine the worst case scenario. We need to start looking at our future in the best case scenario.**

are loved. It reminds us that we have eternal life, that we are protected, and that we are not alone. We are much better off when we ponder the promises of God rather than filling our minds with the empty promises of the world. The world tells us that we need "things" to make us happy. If we believe that, we will never be happy because we will always think we need one more thing. Be happy with what you have now; be happy with where you are now. If we let situations dictate our happiness, tomorrow will just give us another reason to be unhappy.

There are many believers that have trouble with their minds. Even though we have been redeemed, it doesn't mean we will automatically think in a godly way. Christians are still human and are still affected by the fall of Adam and Eve. But if we follow this verse and think about the great things of life it will help us to rejoice always! Thinking positively will give us a better attitude in our hearts. As I am writing this I am thinking of the Old Hymn "Count Your Blessings." Think about the good things in your life and name them one by one. Most of us could list off several of the following: we have health to walk and talk, we have food daily that we eat, we have been given eternal life in heaven, we have friends and family to enjoy, we have a warm place to lay our head at night, and the list goes on and on. What you think about is very important in your Christian walk. Think about the things that God has provided for you, rather than the things that you don't have.

There is a book by Joyce Meyer called the Battlefield of the Mind. She says in this book, "Satan usually deceives people into thinking that the source of their misery or trouble is something other than what it really is. He wants them to think they are unhappy due to what is going on around them (their circumstances), but the misery is actually due to what is going on inside them (their thoughts)." What she is trying to say here is that we blame our unhappiness on other people because of something that they didn't do for us, or some hurtful thing they did do to us. Or we blame our unhappiness on some situation that we face. But none of these things can make me unhappy if I don't focus on them. A quote that I have always loved is, "10% of life is what happens to us and we have no control over it. 90% of life is how we respond." Most of life is our reaction to life. We become unhappy when we give our constant attention to our problems and let them eat us up. There are

> *Even though we have been redeemed, it doesn't mean we will automatically think in a godly way.*

people who are saved and who are going to heaven, but they are not living the victorious life that Jesus died to give them.

Breaking The Devil's Stronghold In Our Minds

Many people imprison themselves to the hurts and pains that they have experienced. They can't move on from the hurts of life. They carry the hurts with them, leaving them with a pretty dismal future. We need to recognize that our minds store the hurts and the pains of our past. Our minds are like a sponge; they will soak up everything that we see and hear on a daily basis. They are like a video camera storing information for us. What information are we storing today that we might recall later? What are we feeding our minds?

We have a tendency to watch TV for many hours a week, or listen to music that affects us negatively. We often think more about the world…sports, movies, news. We fill our minds with much more of the world, than we do with godly things. Our minds are going to recall the things we focus on the most. I can't memorize a verse from the Bible by looking at it once. My mind just doesn't work that way. But if I study it over and over again, and continually feed my mind with the word of God, I am able to memorize scripture. After doing this, my mind will bring these scriptures to my thoughts throughout the day. If our daily routine is feeding

Thinking The Wrong Thoughts

our minds with the world's message, then we are going to start thinking like the world.

We have all been guilty of paying too much attention to what the world wants us to think about. The Bible says in Ephesians 4:22-24, *"You were taught, with regard to your former way of life, to put off your old self, which is being corrupted by its deceitful desires; to be made new in the attitude of your minds; and to put on the new self, created to be like God in true righteousness and holiness."* This verse tells us that we are to turn our back on our former way of life because it is corrupt by our deceitful desires. How do we turn from the old way of life? It says that we must renew our minds. If your mind is thinking about the things of God, then your words and your actions will follow. If your mind is following the pattern of this world, your words and actions will be worldly. Our mind was part of the fall of Adam. Our mind is warped by sin. It will continually replay the bad thoughts over and over again until we re-train it to think the thoughts of God.

> **Our mind is warped by sin. It will continually replay the bad thoughts over and over again until we re-train it to think the thoughts of God.**

We can decide the thoughts that we think. We are not powerless. We choose whether we will focus on the bad or the good. 2 Corinthians 10:4-5 says, *"The weapons we fight with are not the weapons of the world. On the contrary, they have divine power to demolish strongholds. We demolish arguments and every pretension that sets itself up against the knowledge of God, and we take captive every thought to make it obedient to Christ."* Can you see that Satan likes to set up strongholds in our minds? He knows that if he can control your mind, he can control you. He likes us to keep thinking about the negative things that have happened to us. He likes us to focus on our shortcomings. But we can have victory if we practice what Paul says here. Take your thoughts captive. Test the thoughts that come into your mind. Are they from God, or are they thoughts that the enemy has planted in your mind? There is an easy way to get rid of the enemy's thoughts. Praise God and focus on Him. As Christians, we need to hear the voice of hope and reason that is in Jesus Christ, and not listen to the voices of pain and confusion.

2 Timothy 1:7 says, *"For God hath not given us the spirit of fear; but of power, and of love, and of a sound mind."(KJV)* God has put His Spirit inside of you. His Spirit doesn't open you up to fear, worry, hurt feelings or guilt. God's Spirit gives us a proper outlook on life. His Spirit reveals to us the true reality of each situation. God's Spirit is not fooled by the deceptive thoughts that the enemy plants in you. If you have torment in your mind of any kind, stop and praise God for who He is, and thank Him that He has given you a sound mind. Satan likes to remind you of your sins, and of the things that you don't have, so that you can't feel content. God however, reminds you that you are loved and that you have everything that you need.

The author of a book I am currently reading shared an experience that she had with negative thinking. She used to be so engulfed with negativity that she felt depressed, sad, hurt, and lonely. You name it, she felt it. She thought negative emotion was something a person couldn't control—that it was something a person had to live with. She remembers coming to Christ, and believing that it would automatically change her negative mindset. But it still controlled her. As she learned to have an attitude of praise, she learned to battle those feelings by praising God. The more she praised God, the less those negative feelings found their way into her mind.

We need to break Satan's strongholds by praising God and putting our focus on Him. The bad emotions that we feel are not God's will for your life. God wants to transform your mind and set you free from negative emotions so that you are not tormented by them anymore. Jesus has come to set us free. Ask God to help you renew your mind so that you can gain victory in your life.

> *If you have torment in your mind of any kind, stop and praise God for who He is…and thank Him that He has given you a sound mind.*

I want to close this chapter by taking another quick look at verse 8 in this Philippians passage. Paul says, *"Finally, brothers, whatever is true, whatever is noble, whatever is right, whatever is pure, whatever is lovely, whatever is admirable—if anything is excellent or praiseworthy—think about such things."* There is nothing that I like to ponder greater than the cross and what it means for my life. The cross is just two pieces of wood put together, but up on that cross lays the hope of the world. The cross completely changes my outlook on life. There is no problem I can't handle because of the cross. I don't need to fret about tomorrow, because all of my tomorrows are in the nail-pierced hands of Jesus. I can have peace in my heart and my mind because I know what the cross did for me. This world may have its challenges, but I can meet them with a good attitude because I know that eternal life is waiting for me. Think about such things!

PART 3

Transforming Us To Be Like The King

And we, who with unveiled faces all reflect the Lord's glory, are being transformed into his likeness with ever-increasing glory, which comes from the Lord, who is the Spirit.
2 Corinthians 3:18

CHAPTER 10

Reform Your Lives

An American manufacturer was showing his machine factory to a potential customer from Albania. At noon, when the lunch whistle blew, two thousand men and women immediately stopped work and left the building. "Your workers—they're escaping!" cried the visitor. "You've got to stop them." The American said, "Don't worry; they'll be back." And indeed, at exactly one o'clock the whistle blew again and all the workers returned from their break. When the tour was over, the manufacturer turned to his guest and said, "Well, now, which of these machines would you like to order?" The visitor from Albania said, "Forget the machines. How much do you want for that whistle?"[14]

This Albanian visitor was amazed at what the whistle did in people's lives. When the whistle blew, the people listened. It would be great if it was this way in our spiritual lives—God's Word tells us something and then we completely follow His instructions. But in our own lives, it doesn't seem quite that easy. We have to change our way of thinking and the behaviors that we have had for many years. In Jeremiah 7, we see that God is calling us to reform and start walking in His ways.

¹ This is the word that came to Jeremiah from the LORD: ² "Stand at the gate of the LORD's house and there proclaim this message:

"'Hear the word of the LORD, all you people of Judah who come through these gates to worship the LORD. ³ This is what the LORD Almighty, the God of Israel, says: Reform your ways and your actions, and I will let you live in this place. ⁴ Do not trust in deceptive words and say, "This is the temple of the LORD, the temple of the LORD, the temple of the LORD!"

⁵ If you really change your ways and your actions and deal with each other justly, ⁶ if you do not oppress the alien, the fatherless or the widow and do not shed innocent blood in this place, and if you do not follow other gods to your own harm, ⁷ then I will let you live in this place, in the land I gave your forefathers for ever and ever. ⁸ But look, you are trusting in deceptive words that are worthless.

⁹ "'Will you steal and murder, commit adultery and perjury, burn incense to Baal and follow other gods you have not known, ¹⁰ and then come and stand before me in this house, which bears my Name, and say, "We are safe"—safe to do all these detestable things? ¹¹ Has this house, which bears my Name, become a den of robbers to you? But I have been watching! declares the LORD.

Do Not Be Deceived By An Easy Message

As I read this passage, I feel so sorry for Jeremiah. God has called him to a tough task. We see that in verses 2 and 3 that God called him to stand at the gate of the temple and preach a message for them to reform. People by nature don't want to reform their ways, they want to keep on living how they always have. They want to continue to follow the desires of their hearts. They want to continue following the sinful nature because that leads them to do the things they want to do. But there was Jeremiah, standing at the gate of the temple, telling the people that they have gone astray and that they need to come back to God. This was not a popular message for him to speak. If you read the whole book of Jeremiah, you realize that this message is going to get him thrown into prison. People do not want to hear about what they are doing wrong, and that they need to change anything. "How dare you tell me that I need to reform my ways. Who are you to say that I should look harder at how I am living my life." But Jeremiah's message is very clear, "Shape up or destruction is coming your way."

You can understand what the people were thinking by the words that God chose to speak to them in this passage. The people thought they were safe. In verse 4, God says, "Do not trust in deceptive words and say, 'This is the temple

> *People by nature don't want to reform their ways, they want to keep on living how they always have. They want to continue to follow the desires of their hearts.*

of the Lord, the temple of the Lord, the temple of the Lord!'" The false prophets gave people a false sense of security. They deceived people by telling them that Jerusalem would never be destroyed because God's temple was built there. They didn't think any harm could come to them because they were in the presence of God's dwelling place. But God says not to be deceived. In Jeremiah 6:14 God gives them another warning. He says, *"They dress the wound of my people as though it were not serious. 'Peace, peace,' they say, when there is no peace."* Many false prophets came and said, "You're alright in how you are living your life. You don't have to worry about anything." They spoke of peace, when God says there is no peace. God is saying to the false prophets, "Don't tell them they are living ok when they are not. I'm about to send them into exile and you are prophesying peace to them."

We will always have people around us who will reassure us that how we are living is acceptable. 2 Timothy 4:3 says, *"For the time will come when men will not put up with sound doctrine. Instead, to suit their own desires, they will gather around them a great number of teachers to say what their itching ears want to hear."* If someone doesn't want to live the lifestyle the preacher preaches, they find another church who will tell them that their lifestyle is acceptable. We want people around us who will tell us we are alright, and that we don't need to change anything. I am writing this chapter to say that the way you are living your life may not be alright. You shouldn't listen to the flattery of the world saying you are alright, when God is telling you to shape up or disaster will overtake you. You need to search the Word of God and then look at your life. Do they match up? If not, then reform!

> **You need to search the Word of God and then look at your life. Do they match up? If not, then reform!**

Going To Church Cannot Save You!

I believe God wants this passage to be a wake-up call for us. Just as some found false hope in the temple, some people today find false hope in the church. They believe that they are living correctly because they attend church. But the problem is that they live however they want the rest of the week. The temple of God didn't save Jerusalem from being destroyed, and attending church most definitely will not save you either. Don't think that church attendance is an automatic ticket to heaven. There are too many people who go to church who are not saved. Jesus says in Matthew 7:21, *"Not everyone who says to me, 'Lord, Lord,' will enter the kingdom of heaven, but only he who does the will of my Father who is in heaven."* There are a lot of people who come to church and say Lord, Lord. They sing the songs, give a little money, and listen to the sermon. Then they leave and do not follow the will of God beyond the church doors. Jeremiah's listeners came and worshiped, they even brought the appropriate sacrifices. Yet it didn't change the way they lived their lives. The people took time to come to the temple and worship, but they left and continued to neglect the widow, the orphan, and the fatherless. They continued to steal, murder, and commit adultery. God's message through Jeremiah is this: worship is not simply coming into my temple and going through the motions. Worship is actually living out my commandments every day of the week.

Worshipping God is not a part time thing. Worship is something we do at all times—in the midst of all of our activities throughout the day. If we only practice our faith in God during church on Sunday mornings, our faith is useless. God wants us to walk in a covenant relationship with Him every day. A covenant is an agreement between two parties. Consider the covenant relationship you have with your spouse. You are in that relationship every day. Every moment you are married. You are to be faithful to them at all times, with no exceptions. We are in that kind of relationship with the Lord as well. God made a covenant with Israel, and in this passage, God rebukes them for not living it out. God has also made a covenant with us through the cross of Christ. Jesus went to the cross and died for us, He provided a way for us to have eternal life. Then He laid out our part of the covenant. Jesus sums up the covenant in Matthew 22:37-39. Jesus says, *"'Love the Lord your God with all your heart and with all your soul and with all your mind.' This is the first and greatest commandment. And the second is like it: 'Love your neighbor as yourself.'"* The covenant we made with God at our baptism is not to come and worship Him on Sunday morning for an hour or two. We made a covenant to take up our cross daily and follow Him. Every day, all day, we are in this covenant relationship with God. If we want the eternal life that He promises through the covenant, then we need to live out our part of the covenant. His mercies for us are new every morning; our love for God and people should be new every morning as well.

There were two different kinds of people that came to worship at the temple. One group included people who were true worshippers. They loved the Lord and they lived according to God's Word. These people came to worship God for His greatness, for His healing, for His deliverance, and for His provisions. They saw their need for God. They had a heart for God. There were others who came to the temple who were following other gods. This passage says they sacrificed to Baal, yet they wanted to keep the "rituals" of their faith as well, and sacrifice to the Lord. Maybe we worship other things in our lives, but we still feel the need to go to church so we can fulfill some obligation we feel to God. They came to the temple to worship, but they didn't live out their faith on a daily basis. They didn't walk the talk. They cared nothing about the needy, and they did whatever they could to make their own lives better. Do we go to church just to put in our time? We give God two hours, and then we leave everything we learned or sung about at church and continue to live our same old lives week after week.

> *Worship is something we do at all times—in the midst of all of our activities throughout the day. If we only practice our faith in God during church on Sunday mornings, our faith is useless.*

God says in this Jeremiah passage, "The temple will not save you, sacrifices will not save you. Destruction is waiting for you if you do not reform your ways." That is a message we should stand up and take notice of today. Many people reading this are walking in a faithful covenant relationship with God every day, but some may not be. We need to know without a shadow of a doubt that church doesn't save us. Worshipping God for a couple of hours a week will not save you. Do not be like Jeremiah's listeners and deceive yourself into thinking you are safe and you do not need to change your ways because you are a faithful attendee at church. We need to become a new creation in Christ. We need to heed God's warning. Israel (God's people) did not reform their ways, and Jerusalem was destroyed. If we do not reform our ways, it will be far worse for us, because we face eternal punishment in hell. But Jesus died so we could escape that punishment. It is all about entering into a covenant relationship with Jesus, receiving His sacrifice on the cross, and reforming your life to match His Word.

According to the law, the people were commanded to bring sacrifices to the Lord. But there was something more important to God than sacrifice. It was obedience to Him.

> *God wants us to ask Him for forgiveness—we are commanded to do that. But what He wants more than our confession is for us to obey Him in the first place.*

Psalm 51:16-17 says, *"You do not delight in sacrifice, or I would bring it; you do not take pleasure in burnt offerings. The sacrifices of God are a broken spirit; a broken and contrite heart, O God, you will not despise."* This passage isn't telling us that God is against sacrifices. He just didn't like the nonchalant sacrifices that the people were bringing. They were living however they wanted to, and then their sacrifices were supposed to make it all better. People have a tendency to do the same thing today. People often do whatever they want to do in their lives and then they come before the Lord and ask Him to forgive them. They use confession of sins the same way many people in the Bible used sacrifices. They live for their desires and then come with a half hearted token to God, "Please forgive me." And they know very well, that faced with the same opportunities again, they would make the same decisions. God wants us to ask Him for forgiveness—we are commanded to do that. But what He wants more than our confession is for us to obey Him in the first place.

Can you hear Jeremiah's cry? If necessary, make the tough decision to reform your life and pattern it after the Word of God.

CHAPTER 11

Being Transformed

A family from a remote area was making their first visit to a big city. They checked in to a grand hotel and stood in amazement at the impressive sight. Leaving the reception desk, they came to the elevator entrance. They'd never seen an elevator before, and just stared at it, unable to figure out what it was for. An old lady hobbled towards the elevator and went inside. The door closed. About a minute later, the door opened and out came a stunningly good-looking young woman. Dad couldn't stop staring. Without turning his head he patted his son's arm and said, "Go get your mother, son."[15]

This man was obviously stunned at the transformation the old lady apparently made after getting in the elevator. But this chapter is not about how we need to transform our physical looks by changing our hair color, growing a beard, or having cosmetic surgery. God wants us to be transformed by our hearts and minds. He wants to change the way that we think, the way we act, and the way we talk. God doesn't want us to get a face lift—He wants us to acquire a soul lift. The Lord isn't concerned about your physical appearance, but He is deeply concerned with the condition of your heart. In John chapter 2, we read about a story of transformation.

¹ On the third day a wedding took place at Cana in Galilee. Jesus' mother was there, ² and Jesus and his disciples had also been invited to the wedding. ³ When the wine was gone, Jesus' mother said to him, "They have no more wine."

⁴ "Dear woman, why do you involve me?" Jesus replied. "My time has not yet come."

⁵ His mother said to the servants, "Do whatever he tells you."

⁶ Nearby stood six stone water jars, the kind used by the Jews for ceremonial washing, each holding from twenty to thirty gallons.

⁷ Jesus said to the servants, "Fill the jars with water"; so they filled them to the brim.

⁸ Then he told them, "Now draw some out and take it to the master of the banquet."

They did so, ⁹ and the master of the banquet tasted the water that had been turned into wine. He did not realize where it had come from, though the servants who had drawn the water knew. Then he called the bridegroom aside ¹⁰ and said, "Everyone brings out the choice wine first and then the cheaper wine after the guests have had too much to drink; but you have saved the best till now."

¹¹ This, the first of his miraculous signs, Jesus performed at Cana in Galilee. He thus

revealed his glory, and his disciples put their faith in him.

Jesus Uses Something

First let me give you a little background. This passage is about a wedding, and biblical weddings are not like what we are accustomed to today. Their wedding celebrations could last up to a week, and the family had an obligation to provide food and wine for the guests. To run out of something would be a great embarrassment. They didn't have 20 different types of drinks like we do now. No Pepsi, Diet Pepsi, Coke, Cherry Coke, 7 up and Sprite. This was obviously way before the cola industry took off. They had water and wine. Wine was used in times of celebration, and water would not have been acceptable. I remember that when I was growing up, my Mom and Dad would only let us have soda pop once a week. Every Saturday night it was pizza and soda pop night. Let me just tell you that water would not have been acceptable on Saturday nights in the Litwiller home. You just don't serve water on Saturday nights! Soda pop was better than water. And during this time of feasting in this passage, there was no doubt that wine was better than water. Water would not have

God doesn't want us to get a face lift—He wants us to acquire a soul lift. The Lord isn't concerned about your physical appearance, but He is deeply concerned with the condition of your heart.

been acceptable at this feast. So Jesus uses the water to make it into wine.

That is the definition of transformation. Transformation is to change the nature of one thing into something else. You can't transform something if there is nothing there to begin with. It is not creating something out of nothing; it is changing what is already there to something else. God takes what is already inside of us and He changes it for His purpose. We all have a nature inside of us. Unfortunately, because of the sin of Adam and Eve, that nature inside of us is sinful. But God desires to take that nature and transform it into something good. 2 Corinthians 5:17 says, *"Therefore, if anyone is in Christ, he is a new creation; the old has gone, and the new has come!"* This verse is talking about transforming from living for the world, to living for God. You are taking on a whole new nature. We are wretched, we are dirty, and we are wired to sin because of our sinful nature. But when we allow Him to come into our lives—He puts a desire in our hearts to live for Him.

There may be people reading this who are satisfied with their old nature. Perhaps they don't want to be transformed into what God wants them to be. They may worry that allowing God to transform them into what He wants for them would get them to do things they don't want to do. They may have to worry about having to go to church every week, having to read their Bible, having to serve in the church, and being required to give faithfully to the church. They may be concerned that they won't be able to go drinking, and that they'll have to watch what they say. They may not want to do those things, and might even question how anybody could actually like doing these things—nobody in their right mind actually likes to serve, and give, and deny themselves, right?

A man named Steve remembers when he was first dating his wife Anna. One thing Steve admired about her was her love for sports. Steve loved sports too, but there were two sports he didn't like. The first is bowling—he can't understand the point of the game. You throw a cannon ball down a nice floor and it disappears and it comes back again and you do the same thing over and over again. The game just doesn't make sense to him. Another thing he doesn't like to do is roller-skate: your shoes have four wheels on them and all you do is go around in circles. You never get anywhere. On Steve's first date with Anna, he was so excited. He got to her house and asked, "Where would you like to go tonight?" She said, "do you like bowling?" and she picked up her own bowling ball. Now, he wanted to spent time with her and so he said, "I love bowling." The next week he knocked on her door and asked what would you like to do tonight? You can probably guess where she wanted to go...roller skating. He said, "I love to roller skate."[16]

Steve had two of the best times of his life doing things he didn't think he liked to do. What made the change? It was because of his relationship with Anna. Spiritual transformation has to do with our love for God. If we have love for Him, we are going to want to spend time with Him, even if it means doing something we don't like. In the end, we will enjoy it because we love to be with Him. We will enjoy it because it brings pleasure to the God we serve.

Do Whatever He Tells You

Jesus' mother makes a simple statement in John 2:5, *"Do whatever he tells you."* That is good advice for us today as well. Could you imagine if you were one of the servants and He asked you to fill up the stone jars with water? I don't think they had a wine mix back then! Once they filled up the jar with water, Jesus said to dip some out and give it to the master of the banquet. Wouldn't you have had the desire to tell Jesus that it was just water? Wouldn't you have wanted to tell Him that you knew it was water because you were the one who filled it? It probably wouldn't make sense to follow these instructions. But since they were servants, they did exactly what they were told, even though it didn't make any sense. When they took it to the master of the banquet, he didn't taste water, but wine.

The main point comes back to what Mary said, *"Do whatever he tells you."* Our job as Christians is to do

> **Our job as Christians is to do whatever He tells us even if it doesn't make sense to us.**

whatever He tells us even if it doesn't make sense to us. We aren't told to question His requests simply because we don't understand His logic. Many Christians don't see the harm in doing a few things here or there that are different from what God says. We question what He says because it doesn't make sense based on our outlook. Someone may not understand why they can't go out and get drunk with their friends once in a while. They may think a few times won't hurt anything. They might not understand why they have to remain pure before they get married. There are many other situations that we live out every day in which God's Word tells us something, but living contradictory to His Word may not seem that wrong. We may settle for the water when we could have wine. It is water until we do what God tells us to do and then it transforms into wine.

Don't question God's Word, just do what He says. Servants cannot question their masters. They are supposed to do exactly what they are told to do, even if they don't think it is necessary. Servants do not pick and choose the commands they follow. They follow everything. In today's society we see ourselves more like Jesus' friends, than we do His servants. But we are still His servants and we are called to follow what His Word says. The only way we can be transformed is by doing what He says. If we don't, we will remain like water…not becoming something better that He has planned for us.

This transformation would not have happened if the servants were unwilling to follow Jesus' command of filling the jars with water. It took obedience to a simple, and what seemed to be unnecessary, task for a transformation to take place. I don't get to choose which of Jesus' commands are necessary and which ones can be overlooked. I have to follow all of them. What is it going to take for transformation to come into your life? It takes simple acts of obedience. We don't bring the transformation, we are just obedient and God brings the transformation. We want Him to do mighty things in our lives and be transformed into strong Christians, but often we do not follow some of His simplest commands. He wants us to be strong Christians, but we don't follow what He says. A basketball coach wants the players to be good, but they won't be unless they practice the fundamentals. Transformation comes from God, for it to take full effect, we must embrace it.

Jesus doesn't transform us to be less than what we were before. He transforms us so we can be better. He makes us useable for the purposes

> *What is it going to take for transformation to come into your life? It takes simple acts of obedience.*

He has planned for us. Just like water was not good for the banquet, our sinful nature is not good for a life lived for Him. Transformation means to change. You can't transform and stay the same. Being transformed is not easy. Giving up a nature you have had since birth is hard to do. Paul says in Romans 12:2, *"Do not conform any longer to the pattern of this world, but be transformed by the renewing of your mind. Then you will be able to test and approve what God's will is— his good, pleasing and perfect will."* We must allow Him to come in and have His way in our lives. We are not transformed if we do not hand our lives and our decisions over to Him. He tells us to forgive others, but we choose to hold on to our sinful nature and not forgive. Let Him change our minds and the way we think.

> *Jesus doesn't transform us to be less than what we were before. He transforms us so we can be better. He makes us useable for the purposes He has planned for us.*

Do your decisions come from the old creation or from the new creation you are in Christ? If we are willing to transform our thinking to line up with God's will for our lives, one day He will transform our bodies into a heavenly and perfect body. You will never have a headache, stomach ache, tooth ache, and you will not get any disease. Heaven is going to be a perfect place and we will all have perfect bodies. But those transformed bodies are for people who have transformed minds (those who are a new creation).

There are no shortcuts to transformation. It is about seeing our need for Jesus; without Him we deserve death. No matter how good we think we have lived, each and every one of us deserves hell. When I realize what I deserve, compared to what I receive in Christ, I can't help but live for Him. My heart is so full of gratitude because of what Jesus did on the cross, that it motivates me to live my life for God.

Even though we have this wonderful life available to us, some people choose not to live it out because transformation is a hard process. Think about a caterpillar trying to get out of a cocoon.

A man was watching a butterfly trying to get out of a cocoon, the butterfly struggled and struggled to try to get out. The man watched for an hour and thought he would help the butterfly out. He went over and cut the cocoon to help the butterfly get out. The butterfly got out of the cocoon, but it could not fly. The butterfly needs to struggle to get out of the cocoon. When he does, as he pushes his way through the small opening, there is fluid that goes from his body into his wings to give him the strength to fly.[17]

It can be difficult as we are continually being transformed into the people God would have us be. You may be thinking at times, this is not worth being transformed. But continue to read the Word. Continue to serve the Lord with gladness because you will find that being transformed was definitely worth it. When we are obedient in the situations we face during each day, we are transformed into the likeness of Jesus.

CHAPTER 12

The New Nature

Pests. Bugs and rodents. Even the thought of them makes our skin crawl. But pests find their way into everyone's home at one time or another. The question is, do we hate these pests enough to do what it takes to get rid of them? One survey says that it depends on the type of pests that are in the house. 24% of adults will pay an exterminator to kill spiders. 27% of adults, will pay to annihilate ants. 56% will pay to banish bedbugs. The same percentage, 56% will pay to get rid of mice or rats. 58% will pay to kill cockroaches. When we talk about the bug that can bring the house down, 87% of adults will pay to terminate termites. Notice that except for termites, almost half of adults will live with some very unpleasant creatures rather than pay a professional to ensure the pests are eradicated. This survey also showed that many people are willing to endure a certain kind of pest, but not others. Take that concept to a spiritual dimension and the same thing holds true. Many people are willing to live, or feel they have to live, with spiritual ants, spiritual spiders, spiritual cockroaches, spiritual rats, or spiritual termites.[18]

    We are willing to tolerate some of our own sins, and

there are some sins we won't tolerate. There are some sins that we will work hard to get out of our lives. There are other sins that we have allowed to infiltrate our lives, and we allow them to stay. The Apostle Paul says in Ephesians 4 that we need to get rid of them all.

> *[17] So I tell you this, and insist on it in the Lord, that you must no longer live as the Gentiles do, in the futility of their thinking. [18] They are darkened in their understanding and separated from the life of God because of the ignorance that is in them due to the hardening of their hearts. [19] Having lost all sensitivity, they have given themselves over to sensuality so as to indulge in every kind of impurity, with a continual lust for more.*
>
> *[20] You, however, did not come to know Christ that way. [21] Surely you heard of him and were taught in him in accordance with the truth that is in Jesus. [22] You were taught, with regard to your former way of life, to put off your old self, which is being corrupted by its deceitful desires; [23] to be made new in the attitude of your minds; [24] and to put on the new self, created to be like God in true righteousness and holiness.*
>
> *[25] Therefore each of you must put off falsehood and speak truthfully to his neighbor, for we are all members of one body. [26] "In*

your anger do not sin": Do not let the sun go down while you are still angry, ²⁷ and do not give the devil a foothold. ²⁸ He who has been stealing must steal no longer, but must work, doing something useful with his own hands, that he may have something to share with those in need.

²⁹ Do not let any unwholesome talk come out of your mouths, but only what is helpful for building others up according to their needs, that it may benefit those who listen. ³⁰ And do not grieve the Holy Spirit of God, with whom you were sealed for the day of redemption. ³¹ Get rid of all bitterness, rage and anger, brawling and slander, along with every form of malice. ³² Be kind and compassionate to one another, forgiving each other, just as in Christ God forgave you.

Caught Up In The Teaching Of The World

Paul begins this passage firm in his approach to the Ephesus church. Verse 17 says, *"So I tell you this, and insist on it in the Lord, that you must no longer live as the Gentiles do, in the futility of their thinking."* Paul says that he <u>insists</u> on it, in the Lord, that they were no longer supposed to live like the Gentiles. Who were the Gentiles? They were the people who did not have the law; they were the people who did not have a relationship with God. They did not know how to live in a pleasing way before God. As I look at this passage, it is like Paul is telling us today, "Do not live like the people of the world, these people do not know how to live a pleasing life before God." Why live like the world? The world is living by what makes sense to them, and what is acceptable by their own opinion. They are not living by the truth of God's Word.

This was a huge deal to Paul. Just before this passage, Paul was praying that the church of Ephesus would become mature and have knowledge of the truth. In verses 13-14 it says, *"Until we all reach unity in the faith and in the knowledge of the Son of God and become mature, attaining to the whole measure of the fullness of Christ.* Then (Notice the word "then" in this passage. After you have become mature and have knowledge...) *Then we will no longer be infants, tossed back and forth by the waves, and blown here and there by every wind of teaching and by the cunning and craftiness of men in their deceitful scheming."* The Apostle Paul sees a huge problem in the Ephesus church and it is the same problem that we see in the church today. The world's thinking is penetrating itself into the church. We are tossed back and forth in our thinking because we don't know the truth. The world's wisdom seems logical, and leads us to question how any one thing we are doing could hurt anybody. That sounds

> **The world's thinking is penetrating itself into the church. We are tossed back and forth in our thinking because we don't know the truth.**

a lot like Adam and Eve in the garden. Eating this little piece of fruit will not hurt anything. Yet because they ate the fruit, one of their sons killed the other. Because they ate the fruit, look at our world today. There are wars, murders, rapes, child molesting, homosexuality, and sexual immorality of all kinds. We hear Satan's voice in our heads saying that what we are doing is not that bad. We get tossed back and forth, unsure of what we should believe in our lives. Paul says we should know the truth and not get caught up in the craftiness of the world.

In verses 18-19 Paul continues to talk about the world. He says, *"They are darkened in their understanding and separated from the life of God because of the ignorance that is in them due to the hardening of their hearts. Having lost all sensitivity, they have given themselves over to sensuality so as to indulge in every kind of impurity, with a continual lust for more."* These verses tell us about how the world lives. Do you see the words Paul uses here? They are separated from the life of God, they have hardened hearts, they give into sensuality, and they have a continual lust for more. The world lives in opposition to God! They are hard hearted to His truth. All they care about is getting what they want, when they want it. The world doesn't care about what God says is right or wrong, they just have a continual lust to get more things for themselves. We need to see that Paul is warning the Ephesus church not to live like the world. That is the same warning he would have for us today. Be set apart from the world.

We Were Taught The Truth Of God's Word

We just saw Paul talking about how the world chooses to live. Now he says in verses 20-21, *"You, however, did not come to know Christ that way. Surely you heard of him and were taught in him in accordance with the truth that is in Jesus."* You did not come to know Christ by the ways of the world. You came to know Christ by the truth…by the Word of God. If you came to know Christ through the truth, why would you want to live your life by the world's teaching?

Paul goes on to remind us of what we were taught. Verse 22-24 says, *"You were taught, with regard to your former way of life, to put off your old self, which is being corrupted by its deceitful desires; to be made new in the attitude of your minds; and to put on the new self, created to be like God in true righteousness and holiness."* We were all taught to get rid of our former self; our former life. We all were like the Gentiles, like the world, lost in our sins because we did not know the truth. But now that we have come to know the truth in Jesus Christ, Paul tells us, "Put off your old self, and put on the new self." It is an action that we must take, like putting on clothes each day. We don't wake up each day and dig through the dirty clothes hamper to find something to wear (at least I hope we don't). We put on the new, not the old. Why would you want to wear something that is stained or smelly, when you have something fresh to wear? That is Paul's question to us. In Romans 13:14, he says, *"Rather, clothe yourselves with the Lord Jesus Christ, and do not think about how to gratify the desires of the sinful nature."* Each day spiritually,

The New Nature

we can go to the dirty hamper and wear our same old sinful self, or we can put on the new clothes that we have in Jesus Christ. If you were going on a date with someone you really loved, would you wear a stained or smelly shirt from the clothes hamper? No way. You wouldn't even think of it! So why do we choose to come before God, whom I hope we love, wearing our filthy clothes of sin?

2 Corinthians 5:17 says, *"Therefore, if anyone is in Christ, he is a new creation; the old has gone, and the new has come!"* Our new self looks completely different than the old self. There

> *Each day spiritually, we can go to the dirty hamper and wear our same old sinful self, or we can put on the new clothes that we have in Jesus Christ.*

hasn't been a change physically in the way we look. Physically we are the same people, but inside, our hearts and thoughts are completely different.

In the movie "Air Force One", Harrison Ford plays the President of the United States. At the end of the movie, the President's plane, Air Force One, was about to crash into the Ocean. Another military plane was right beside them and they stretched a wire between the two planes to get people off Air Force One. People in Washington DC were anxiously waiting to hear if the President got off of Air Force One before it crashed into the ocean. The last one to cross the wire into the military plane was the President. And when he was safely on board the military plane, the pilot reported to Washington DC. "Liberty 2-4 has now become Air Force One!" Did the plane change? No. What changed was who was inside the plane. The presence of the President made the military plane Air Force One. When Jesus comes into our lives, do we suddenly have a new body? No, but Him coming into us, changes our identity. That military plane is not going to be sent into battle with the President on board. The military plane's identity changed; they are getting out of the fight and getting the President back home safely. When Jesus comes in, we are changed, we are a new creation. We don't live the same lives we use to, we live by the truth that we are taught.

God Desires A Change In How We Live

In the rest of this Ephesians 4 passage, from verses 25-32, are many different ways that God calls us to be different after being clothed with Jesus. We don't live like the world, we don't live like our old selves…we start to live like Jesus. Verse 27 says, *"and do not give the devil a foothold."* All the devil needs is a foothold. If he can get his foot in the door, you will not be able to shut it. Once he has a foothold, then he will continue to wear you down and gradually the door will be opened more and more to him. When Jesus comes into our lives, we should shut the door on the devil. I am not even going to give the devil an opportunity to do anything in my life, because if you give him an inch he will take a mile. He will overstep the boundaries that you give him. That is why we

> *When Jesus comes into our lives, we should shut the door on the devil. I am not even going to give the devil an opportunity to do anything in my life.*

do not surrender any ground to our crafty enemy! He will take more than what you give him.

These verses don't give us an exhausted list of how we should live our lives, but they give us examples of ways that we are to be different. We are to talk differently, we are to get rid of all anger, we are to be kind and compassionate, and we are to be quick to forgive. When we don't do these things and live our lives against what God's word teaches, look at what happens in verse 30. *"And do not grieve the Holy Spirit of God, with whom you were sealed for the day of redemption."* Are we grieving the Holy Spirit by the way we talk, the way we hold bitterness, or how we are slow to forgive? Do we grieve the Holy Spirit by the way we choose to live our lives? Some people may think that God is some object out there that has no feelings, and therefore we can't grieve Him. But look at the Bible. God created us and died for us because He wanted <u>our fellowship</u>. The Bible says <u>He is a jealous God</u> when we choose other things over Him. We grieve Him when we choose not to live for Him and take on His character in our lives.

It is not enough just to have an absence of sin in your life; you also must work to do good deeds. Verse 28 says, *"He who has been stealing must steal no longer, but must work, doing something useful with his own hands, that he may have something to share with those in need."* This verse says that not only are we supposed to stop stealing, but we are to work to help people who are in need. The absence of sin is not enough, but we need to have a desire to be used in the kingdom of God. In verse 29 we see the same principle apply,

"Do not let any unwholesome talk come out of your mouths, but only what is helpful for building others up according to their needs, that it may benefit those who listen." Obviously we are to stop using our speech to tear others down, but does that mean we are never to say anything again? No, we are supposed to use our speech to build other people up. The bad is not just taken away, but it is replaced with good. You get rid of the sins of the flesh and you replace it with the fruit of the Spirit.

There is a story about a man who refused to clean up all his junk in his yard… Refusing to clean up his own backyard landed George Hartsuff in jail for 60 days. He can't say he wasn't warned. City officials had been asking him to do a little cleaning since 2000. Court action to ensure compliance was taken in 2002. On July 5, 2007, authorities gave Hartsuff 30 days to clean out the boats, crab pots, vending machines, and other assorted debris that littered his Maryland yard. When he failed to do so entirely, he was sentenced to 60 days in prison. Hartsuff and his lawyer insisted they were doing their best to tidy things up. They had already hauled away four 30-yard dumpsters, filled to capacity. Still, city officials and authorities were fed-up. The county spokesperson said, "This cycle will keep going until the property is cleaned up. The site would get cleaned a bit, and it got messy again…it was never brought into compliance."[19]

Could that describe us? We all have a lot of junk in our lives, and we are unwilling to clean it up. We get rid of a little sin here and there thinking we are sacrificing for the Lord, but all the while we bring more sin into our lives. I will use the words of the county spokesperson in this story, "We need to come to compliance, to the point that we surrender our lives to the Lordship of Christ. Otherwise our backyard will always be a mess."

Ephesians 5:1 is one verse after the particular passage that we looked at in this chapter. It says, *"Be imitators of God, therefore, as dearly loved children."* That is the goal that every Christian should be striving for. I want to imitate God. I want to speak what He would speak, I want to forgive like He would forgive, and I want to live like He would live. A goal of every disciple is to look like their teacher.

> *"We need to come to compliance, to the point that we surrender our lives to the Lordship of Christ. Otherwise our backyard will always be a mess."*

CHAPTER 13

Be In The World—Not Of It

Have you ever felt dirty, broken, or worthless? Everyone has. But if someone offered you a $20 bill, would you take it? What if that person wadded it up and threw it on the ground—would you still want it? What if they stepped on it, kicked it, and even spit on it? Could you still go to the store and spend it? The answer to each of these questions is yes. That bill has value because of what it is, not because of how it looks, where it's been, or what it's been used for. A crisp, clean, $20 bill is worth the same amount as an ugly, older, more used one. You may feel like you've been stepped on, beat up, or kicked around. You may feel dirty, unworthy, or useless. But be encouraged by the $20 bill—no matter what you've been through, you still have value to God![20]

Maybe some people feel like a dirty crumbled up $20 bill. The way you lived your life would make a sailor blush. You think to yourself, "How in the world can I be accepted by God?" Well, no matter what you have done in your past, you do have value to God. You are just as valuable to God as the crisp $20 bill; just as valuable as someone who didn't have the wild life. This is also a good reminder for those who are confident in themselves because of the "good" life they have lived. You may be a crisp $20 bill, but your value in God's sight is the same as a repentant dirty old crumbled up $20 bill. Paul tells us in Philippians 3, not to put confidence in ourselves and our works.

> *¹ Finally, my brothers, rejoice in the Lord! It is no trouble for me to write the same things to you again, and it is a safeguard for you.*
> *² Watch out for those dogs, those men who do evil, those mutilators of the flesh. ³ For it is we who are the circumcision, we who worship by the Spirit of God, who glory in Christ Jesus, and who put no confidence in the flesh— ⁴ though I myself have reasons for such confidence.*
> *If anyone else thinks he has reasons to put confidence in the flesh, I have more: ⁵ circumcised on the eighth day, of the people of Israel, of the tribe of Benjamin, a Hebrew of Hebrews; in regard to the law, a Pharisee; ⁶ as for zeal, persecuting the church; as for legalistic righteousness, faultless.*
> *⁷ But whatever was to my profit I now consider loss for the sake of Christ. ⁸ What is more, I consider everything a loss compared to the surpassing greatness of knowing Christ Jesus my Lord, for whose sake I have lost all things. I consider them rubbish, that I may*

gain Christ [9] and be found in him, not having a righteousness of my own that comes from the law, but that which is through faith in Christ— the righteousness that comes from God and is by faith. [10] I want to know Christ and the power of his resurrection and the fellowship of sharing in his sufferings, becoming like him in his death, [11] and so, somehow, to attain to the resurrection from the dead.

We Are Not To Put Confidence In Ourselves

Many people put confidence in themselves to do anything that they put their mind to. And when it comes to salvation, many people think they can attain that for themselves as well. "If *I* do the right things—I will be saved." Paul was facing this type of thinking in Philippi. Philippi was a Gentile town who accepted the message that it is by Jesus that you are saved. However, some Jews came along and said this is not entirely so. They declared that they needed to be circumcised also. Many Jews accepted Jesus, but they still held to the fact that they still had to do certain things to be saved. They believed that Jesus plus circumcision saves you. Paul wrote this letter to the Philippian church to let them know that this is false thinking. It isn't Jesus plus anything that saves you. It is just Jesus.

It isn't Jesus plus anything that saves you. It is just Jesus.

Jesus said on the cross that it is finished. You can't add anything to your salvation. Salvation doesn't come by your good acts. Paul sends out a warning not to listen to people who say you are saved by what you do.

In this passage Paul uses the strongest language I can recall him using. He calls his opponents dogs, mutilators of the flesh, and evil doers. Paul has some strong words against them because they are misrepresenting the gospel. Paul was strong with his words because there was a big danger of people following this particular teaching of adding to what Jesus did. Many people today think the same thing. Jesus died, but I also have to do this and that to be saved. Here is a story that shows that our value comes from Jesus alone.

There was a man who had a small collection of baseball cards. The card that is worth the most is called "Future Stars" and is valued at $100. Future stars—people to watch because they are going to be good. This card is over 20 years old. There are three players on this card. The first is Jeff Schneider. How many people have heard of Jeff Schneider? Schneider played 1 year of professional baseball, pitched in 11 games, and gave up 13 earned runs in those 11 games. The second player is Bobby Bonner. How many people have heard of Bobby Bonner? He played 4 years of baseball but only appeared in 61 games, with 8 runs batted in, and 0 home runs. The third "Future Star" was Cal Ripken Jr. Cal played 21 years for the Baltimore Orioles and appeared in

3,001 games. He came to bat 11,551 times, collected 3,184 hits and 431 home runs, and batted in 1,695 runs. He set a major league record for most consecutive games started. Now imagine if you met Bobby Bonner, and he shook your hand and boasted, "Did you know that my baseball card is worth over $100?" You would laugh because you know the worth of the card has nothing to do with him. It is all about being on the same card as Cal Ripken Jr. That's how it is when we come to Christ and point to our good works, our statistics, "Look how good I am…How much I'm worth." If you want to hold up your stats to God, you don't have a chance. But when you put your faith in Christ, your baseball card (or life) is worth a lot because of someone else's stats (Jesus).[21]

There are two general categories in religion. The religions that require specific actions…and the ones that say it has been done. Christianity is different from any other religion because Christianity says it is done. As Jesus was dying on the cross, He said, "It is finished." You cannot add to your salvation. We see a huge switch in Paul's life once he figures this out. He still continues to do mighty things in his life for God, but it is no longer about him. He doesn't stop serving and obeying God when he finds out that his works don't save him. He serves God even more. What Jesus did for him motivates him to serve. Paul used to be focused on self—what he did. Now it boils down to what Jesus did for him. Paul says in verse 7, *"But whatever was to my profit I now consider loss for the sake of Christ."* Is that saying what he did was wrong? No. He was circumcised, he was a man committed to the law of God—that stuff is not wrong. It is wrong however, to make that your motive of salvation. We can get caught up in our works as well. Someone may go to church every week, help out at youth group, serve on the board, and teach Sunday school. Look at all they do. That stuff is not wrong, it is great they do those things for the Lord—but that stuff does not add to their salvation.

> *We can't earn the un-earnable! Salvation is a gift. Our works are just expressions of thanks for that gift.*

We can't earn the un-earnable! Salvation is a gift. Our works are just expressions of thanks for that gift. You can probably correlate how thankful you are for your salvation by the works that you do. The more thankful you are, the more you want to give back to God.

Our Desire Should Be To Know Jesus

Paul says whatever was to my profit I consider loss for the sake of Christ, he then adds to that statement in verse 8, *"What is more, I consider everything a loss compared to the surpassing greatness of knowing Christ Jesus my Lord, for whose sake I have lost all things. I consider them rubbish, that I may gain Christ."* Paul has come to know Jesus, and he realizes there is nothing else in life that even comes close to that. "Everything is a loss compared to knowing Christ." Compared to knowing Jesus—why should it matter what house we live in, or the car that we drive? We shouldn't be concerned with the amount of money we make, or whether or not we are the most popular person at our job or church. We shouldn't care because we know Jesus.

Again, Paul uses a strong word here, "rubbish". I consider everything rubbish compared to Jesus. I think of it as garbage. Not many of us think of our brand new cars or large screen TV's as garbage. But place them next to Jesus and that is what they look like. If you are truly focused upon Christ, worldly things start to lose their sparkle. Paul had a huge shift in his world view here. What was once most important to him has now been changed. The greatest thing to him after this realization was to know Jesus.

> *Compared to knowing Jesus—why should it matter what house we live in, or the car that we drive? We shouldn't be concerned with the amount of money we make, or whether or not we are the most popular person at our job or church. We shouldn't care because we know Jesus.*

What does it mean to know someone? You could ask me if I know the President of the United States. Yes, I know him. He is Barak Obama. His wife is Michelle Obama. He has two kids Malia and Shasha. He is from Chicago, Illinois, which is my home state. Before he was President, he was the Senator from Illinois. He is left handed and he has won the Nobel Peace Prize. I can rattle off many more facts about our President by reading a book about him. But just because I know these facts about him doesn't mean I know him. I don't have the first clue about who he really is just because I know some facts about his life. I will always remember what my seminary professors said, "We are not called to know of God...but to know God." It is not about intellectually knowing who He is, but experiencing Him. The more time you spend with someone, the better you will know them. It is that simple. Some people comment, "I wish I had as much faith and trust in God as 'so-and-so' has." Well if you spent as much time with God as they do, then you probably would have that kind of strong faith. In *The Purpose Driven Life* book, Rick Warren says, "There are no short cuts to spiritual maturity." You need to put in the time. If you don't have a strong, committed relationship with God, it's likely that you haven't put in the time to work on that relationship. A good relationship takes time.

When Paul writes about knowing God in this verse, he is not just talking intellectually. Would intellectually knowing someone be enough in the other relationships you have? When you are dating, you have a passion and desire to know more about the other person. You would not be content having someone else tell you a bunch of factual information about her. "She went to work today and accomplished a lot. After work she went to the grocery store to buy food for supper. She ate supper and then met up with a couple of friends to go see a movie. She came home and read a book for an hour before she went to bed." You would not be content with just the facts of what took place in her day; you would want to be a part of it. You would want to talk with her and experience what she had to say.

We should not be content in "knowing" God, or knowing the facts of who He is. We should have a passion and desire to experience Him in our lives. Paul goes on to say in verse 10, *"I want to know Christ and the power of his resurrection and the fellowship of sharing in his sufferings, becoming like him in his death."* He was not content with knowledge, he wanted to experience Jesus—His sufferings and His resurrection. After experiencing Jesus and seeing how great He is, Paul was willing to lose everything he had. Not only was he willing, but he did lose everything. How much are we willing to lose for Christ?

> When Texas pastor Jim Denison was in college, he served as a summer missionary in East Malaysia. While there he attended a small church. At one of the church's worship services, a teenage girl came forward to announce her decision to follow Christ and be baptized. During the service, Denison noticed some worn-out luggage leaning against the wall of the church building. He asked the pastor about it. The pastor pointed to the girl who had just been baptized and told Denison, "Her father said that if she was baptized as a Christian she could never go home again. So she brought her luggage."[22]

This is a powerful story about leaving it all to follow Christ. I am sure that there are not too many people reading this book who have had to make that kind of sacrifice to follow Jesus. Would you be willing to give up everything for Jesus?

> *Too often we are not willing to sacrifice a Starbucks coffee to know Jesus through giving. Too often we refuse to shut off the TV to spend an hour in communion with the Lord. Or we just get too focused on our lives that we are too busy to know God through serving in His Kingdom.*

Verse 8 says, *"What is more, I consider everything a loss compared to the surpassing greatness of knowing Christ Jesus my Lord, for whose sake I have lost all things. I consider them rubbish, that I may gain Christ."* Too often we are not willing to sacrifice a Starbucks coffee to know Jesus through giving. Too often we refuse to shut off the TV to spend an hour in communion with the Lord. Or we just get too focused on our lives that we are too busy to know God through serving in His Kingdom. "I want to know you Lord, but let me take care of some other things first. I will get to know you better Lord when this TV show is over. I will serve you more when this project at work is over. I will get to know you better by increasing my giving as soon as I get my next raise." TV shows come and go and the Bible is still rarely opened. Projects at work are finished, yet we find other ways to spend our free time. We get our raises, but find other things to spend our money on. Lord, help us all to want to know you better.

As we strive to be in the world, and not of it, we need to have a new mindset. We need to make the decision to follow Jesus and deny our selfish desires. We must take the focus off of ourselves, and our desires. The Lord must become our focus! We should desire Him more than anything that this world can offer.

> *We need to make the decision to follow Jesus and deny our selfish desires. We must take the focus off of ourselves, and our desires. The Lord must become our focus!*

CHAPTER 14

Our View Of Sin

The late President Calvin Coolidge returned home from attending church early one Sunday afternoon. His wife had been unable to attend, but she was interested in what the minister spoke on in the service. Coolidge responded, "Sin." She pressed him for a few words of explanation. And being a man of few words with his wife, he responded, "Well, I think he was against it."[23]

Christians are against sin, but it is something that every Christian does from time to time. No one has it mastered. Jesus was the only one who lived without committing one sin. I define sin as disobedience to God. Whether it is something we do when we know we shouldn't, or something we don't do that we know we should. Both are disobedience to God. Whether we want to or not, we have to deal with sin. But a Christian views his sin differently than someone who does not follow the Lord. We desire to get rid of sin in our lives because it only causes anguish. Romans 7 is a passage I have gone back to many times in my life.

[14] *We know that the law is spiritual; but I am*

unspiritual, sold as a slave to sin. ¹⁵ I do not understand what I do. For what I want to do I do not do, but what I hate I do. ¹⁶ And if I do what I do not want to do, I agree that the law is good. ¹⁷ As it is, it is no longer I myself who do it, but it is sin living in me. ¹⁸ I know that nothing good lives in me, that is, in my sinful nature. For I have the desire to do what is good, but I cannot carry it out. ¹⁹ For what I do is not the good I want to do; no, the evil I do not want to do—this I keep on doing. ²⁰ Now if I do what I do not want to do, it is no longer I who do it, but it is sin living in me that does it.

²¹ So I find this law at work: When I want to do good, evil is right there with me. ²² For in my inner being I delight in God's law; ²³ but I see another law at work in the members of my body, waging war against the law of my mind and making me a prisoner of the law of sin at work within my members. ²⁴ What a wretched man I am! Who will rescue me from this body of death? ²⁵ Thanks be to God—through Jesus Christ our Lord!

So then, I myself in my mind am a slave to God's law, but in the sinful nature a slave to the law of sin.

A Christian's Struggle With Sin

Struggling with sin is not a new thing that God's people have started to deal with over the last few years. Throughout the ages, all of God's people have struggled with sin. I like to point out to people how much of the Bible deals with sin. In Genesis 1 and 2 there is no sin in the world. In Revelation 21 and 22 refers to the time when we are in heaven, where there is also no sin. In the first two chapters at the beginning of the Bible, and in the last two chapters at the end, there is no sin. However, everything else in the Bible is about fallen man and his struggle to live in obedience to God.

> *Each time that we are able to claim a victory over temptation it helps us build momentum to win future battles. Every temptation that we lose makes it easier to give in the next time.*

King David was called "A man after God's own heart." Yet even David made some very bad choices which led him into many different kinds of sin. In this passage, we see that Paul struggled with sin in his life. This chapter is not written for us to come to the conclusion that everyone sins, and that it is not a big deal. It is a big deal! We are to be striving to take sin out of our lives. Look at how Paul, David, and other godly people dealt with their sins. They felt terrible and repented of them. We will struggle with sin, but don't just give up and give into sin. Each time that we are able to claim a victory over temptation it helps us build momentum to win future battles. Every temptation that we lose makes it easier to give in the next time. We will face the same battles, the same temptations over and over again until we claim victory.

When we read about Paul's life, we remember that he was once a harsh man. He went from town to town arresting and killing Christians. We can see by his lifestyle that Paul was definitely a sinner at one point. But surely after Paul's conversion, he left his life of sin and began to follow Christ, right? Paul definitely did change his life, but even though he left his wicked ways, he still struggled with sin. This Romans 7 passage is not about his old lifestyle, it is about a committed Christian stumbling and falling. In this passage Paul doesn't use the past tense to describe his old lifestyle, but he uses the present tense to describe his current position. There is a battle raging inside of Paul. It is a battle between the sinful nature and the Spirit of God that lives in him.

As I read this passage I feel good that the Apostle Paul wrestled with sin. Not because I'm happy he had to struggle, but because it shows that mature Christians <u>do</u> struggle with sin. I am not the only one struggling with the sinful nature inside of me. Stop and think about the godly man that Paul was. He wrote over half of the New Testament. He was beaten many times for his faith, he was stoned, he was put into prison on several occasions, and eventually he gave his life for the name of Jesus. Yet this great man of God struggled with sin in his life just like you and I do. We are not alone in our struggle with sin.

There is a war taking place inside each believer. Paul

Yet this great man of God struggled with sin in his life just like you and I do. We are not alone in our struggle with sin.

says in Galatians 5:17, *"For the sinful nature desires what is contrary to the Spirit, and the Spirit what is contrary to the sinful nature. They are in conflict with each other, so that you do not do what you want."* We have this fallen nature inside of us that was handed down to us from Adam and Eve. As long as we are in our earthly bodies, we are going to have to fight this sinful nature that wants what is contrary to our new nature in Christ.

> A grandfather was talking to his grandson. "Grandson," he said, "there are two wolves living in my heart and they are at war with each other. One is vicious and cruel, the other is loving and kind." "Grandfather," said the alarmed grandson, "which one will win?" The grandfather paused before he said, "The one I feed."[24]

This sinful nature is stronger in some people than it is in others because they continue to feed it a steady diet. Some people are tired of the war that is taking place inside of them and they just give in to the sinful nature. They are tired of trying to be good. They feel as though they can't do it. They are frustrated by the results.

I detest the sin that is in my life. I wish all I had to do was accept Jesus as my Savior and the sin would vanish from my life. But unfortunately, in my frail humanity, I will never conquer sin on this earth. There is a quote that says, "There is an eagle in me that wants to soar, and there is a hippopotamus in me that wants to wallow in the mud."[25] Too often we wallow in the mud when we could be soaring in the sky. We need to get serious about fighting the sinful nature inside of us because it will just lead us floundering in the mud.

> **This sinful nature is stronger in some people than it is in others because they continue to feed it a steady diet.**

As Christians, do we see the ugliness of sin that is in our lives? We may look at our lives and see sin, but we may say to ourselves, "My sin is not that bad." You look at others and they have more sin in their lives than you do. Paul didn't take his sin lightly. In the letter Paul wrote to his young friend Timothy, Paul says in 1 Timothy 1:15, *"Here is a trustworthy saying that deserves full acceptance: Christ Jesus came into the world to save sinner— of whom I am the worst."* He says that he was the worst of sinners. Paul did have a checkered past, but there would have been many more people who were worse than he was. Paul was not comparing his sin to others as he made this statement. No, as Paul approached God, he simply despised the sin that he had in his life.

Jesus shares a parable in Luke 18 of the Pharisee and the Tax Collector. In that parable, the Pharisee went to pray and said how thankful he was that he wasn't like the tax collector. "I am glad I am not like that sinner over there." And the tax collector went to pray and showed remorse for the sins that he had in his life. He prayed, "God, have mercy on me, a sinner." He didn't try to justify himself before God. The Pharisee listed all of the good things that he had done that others didn't do. The Pharisee might have lived a better life than the tax collector, but he still had sin in His life. He didn't think his sin was a big deal because he lived a better life than most people. The lesson that we need to see is—Even if we live better than most people, even if we have only one sin (which we have a lot more than one sin in our lives), we need to repent of that sin. It does me no good that I am less of a sinner than someone else. What matters is that I have sinned! If I have sinned once, I deserve the same thing as the person who has sinned 1 million times. We both deserve death. We deserve hell's eternal fire. In the garden, Adam and Eve only committed one sin. The result of that one sin was death. It is not the 100th or 1000th sin that causes death. It is the first. Sin separates us from God. God is holy and cannot have sin in His presence.

When Paul saw his sin, it really bothered him. He felt the conviction of the Holy Spirit because of the sin in his life. The Holy Spirit's job is to convict us when we walk contrary to the Lord. If you sin and you don't feel convicted, that is when you need to start to worry. Is the Holy Spirit really living in you if you are not convicted of your sin? The Holy Spirit prompted Paul to feel bad about his sins. Look at what Paul calls himself in Romans 7:24. *"What a wretched man I am! Who will rescue me from this body of death?"* Paul shows us his weakness here. Usually he is the strong father figure encouraging his converts to live devoted lives for God. But here he totally admits that he struggles like any other person in the area of sin. He doesn't see himself as spiritually perfect or towering over everyone else in the faith. No, he says that he is a wretched man—that the sin in his life brings death to his body—that he needs rescuing. Have we come to honest terms with how bad we are without Jesus Christ? Do you see yourself like Paul? As the worst of sinners; a wretch? Paul knew he was incomplete by himself and that he needed to be rescued. Test yourself of this today. Can you say yes to these three statements:

1. I am a sinner. Romans 3:23
2. I know my sin deserves death. Romans 6:23. I recognize I deserve hell.
3. As a Christian I feel the conviction of the Holy Spirit when I sin.

A Christian should not be content or have peace if they are living with unrepented sin in their lives.

It does me no good that I am less of a sinner than someone else. What matters is that I have sinned!

As a strong believer in the Lord, are you like the Apostle Paul? Are you engaged in the struggle to put your flesh in its place? I encourage you to feed the spirit and starve the sinful nature.

A Christian's Answer To Sin Is Jesus

This passage shows us the battle that takes place and how the sinful nature sometimes gets the best of us. In verse 24, Paul says, *"What a wretched man I am! Who will rescue me from this body of death?"* Paul took his sin seriously. He detested his sin. Some people see sin in their life and say, "Everybody sins, it is no big deal." Paul says, "What a wretched man I am!" He couldn't stand the things he saw himself do. Some people may have looked at Paul's sin and said, "Paul, you're not that bad. Don't worry about that. Other people are far worse than you." But he knew it was bad. He wasn't going to try to justify his sin. He wasn't going to let the people of the world tell him that his sin was not that bad. He recognized that his sin was rebellion against God.

Paul then asked the question, *"Who will rescue me from this body of death?"* This is a rhetorical question. Paul knew the answer. Verse 25, *"Thanks be to God—through Jesus Christ our Lord!"* Paul saw this condition in him that was not good, but he knew who could rescue him. The wages of sin is death. But what Jesus did on the cross rescues us from our body of death. I am alive in Christ. Jesus took my death so I can live.

> **He wasn't going to let the people of the world tell him that his sin was not that bad. He recognized that his sin was rebellion against God.**

Paul continued his thoughts into Romans 8. Verse 1 says, *"Therefore, there is now no condemnation for those who are in Christ Jesus."* The central theme of the passage that we studied in this chapter is that the law doesn't save us from spiritual death. The law just points out the fact that we are dying. It is Jesus that comes and rescues us. As we commit sins in our lives, we may feel condemnation. Satan is telling you, "How can you be a Christian and yet do that. You might as well stop trying to be a Christian." We may believe Satan, because we are kicking ourselves for making poor decisions. But I challenge you to see the victory we have in Jesus, even when we do disobey.

There was a man who looked at the trees up on a hill and he couldn't understand why the trees leaned to the west. He said to a friend, "There are several times a year when the wind blows 50-80 miles an hour towards the east pushing these trees. You would think that these trees would be leaning to the east because of these heavy winds." His friend responded, "Yes, several times a year the wind does blow really hard towards the east, but it is the gentle west winds that blow year around that makes the trees lean to the west."[26]

It is the same way in our lives. Sometimes sin will come into our lives and hit our lives hard. But our lives are not marked by the occasional sin. Our lives are marked by the gentle, continual work of the Holy Spirit. Is your life marked by the gentle work of the Holy Spirit, or does the sinful nature shape your life? Do you live a lifestyle of sin and occasionally show the fruits of the Spirit? Or do you walk in the ways of the Spirit and occasionally get tripped up? Hopefully, when we do get tripped up, there is conviction by the Spirit of God. Let the Holy Spirit convict you, so you can turn back in repentance. Let your life be shaped by the constant blowing of the Holy Spirit over your life!

Conclusion

As you can see we are a mess. We do not deserve to stand in the presence of the King of Kings. Isaiah 64:6 says, *"All of us have become like one who is unclean, and all our righteous acts are like filthy rags..."* Even on our best days, in our best moments, we still have to totally rely on His grace to let us come into His presence. How are we so privileged to stand before Him? It is because of the cross—the great love of our Father God!

> There was a man flying on an airplane and he sat beside a young mother and her one year-old boy. Whenever someone would walk by he would say daddy. It turned out that they were away for a couple days and he was on his way home to see his daddy. The flight was very rough. It was so turbulent that the flight attendants did not get up once the entire trip. The little boy would cry and his mother would soothe him by feeding him. The problem was that the flight was so bumpy that the boy brought more up than he ate. When the time came to get off of the flight, there was a

man dressed in a suit who was trying to be as polite as he could. However, he didn't want to touch the little boy or anything around his seat—because he left a mess. The man got off of the airplane and saw a young man who had to be the father. He was dressed up with nice pants and a white shirt. He assumed the father wouldn't want to hold his son in that outfit. The boy was a mess…and his dad was dressed up. But the man watched as the Father reached out and grabbed his son and hugged and kissed him all the way to the baggage claim. He didn't care about the fact that his son was a mess. He was just glad to have his son back with him.[27]

    This story shows us how strong a father's love can be. The man on the plane didn't even want to come close to this messy little boy. But when the Father saw his son, he didn't care how messy he was. All he wanted to do was hug and kiss him. He couldn't get enough of his son. This is a great picture of God. When we are messy and come to Him full of sin and shame, He doesn't try to avoid us. He welcomes us with open arms. He takes us, hugs and kisses us, and cleans us up.

    In our world today, it is easy to get distracted and find other things to do, rather than standing before our Father, the King of Kings. We get sucked into the "important" situations in our lives and we miss the essential event. There is no greater event than to stand before the King! Don't ever think that a baseball game, waterskiing, picking up an extra shift at work, or whatever else you might have going on is as important as the privilege of standing before our Almighty King.

I encourage you to ponder in your heart the attitude you have towards standing in the King's Presence. What things take priority in your life? What takes you away from spending time in His Presence? The things we do may not be wrong, but what we miss out on is infinitely better.

If you don't have a true desire to be with the King of Kings, I hope this book has made you think. There is no place better to take your petitions, your hurts, your sorrows, your joys…than to the King Himself. Let's go to the King together:

> *Lord Jesus,*
>
> *You are my King! I treasure every opportunity I have to come into Your presence. I do not want to be distracted by the things in my life, in which I forfeit my privilege to stand before you. Help me to prioritize my life and put you first above everything else. Let me be in tune to your voice and not get caught up in the traps the devil has set for me. God, I realize it is difficult to turn away from the sinful nature that I have fed for so long, but I hunger for your Spirit. I want to be made*

new in You. Today I prepare myself as I put myself in a spot to see you...meet me in Your tender mercies. Thank You for holding out Your gold scepter to me as you died upon the cross. Through the cross I can come to my King and not die. I serve no other but You, the King above all Kings. Amen.

ENDNOTES

[1] *"Sammy Sosa's Corked Bat Exposed"*, Gordon MacDonald, author, speaker, Leadership editor-at-large, in Leadership Weekly (7-8-03). (Preachingtoday.com).

[2] *Deceitful Playing"*, Ravi Zacharias, "The Lostness of Humankind," Preaching Today, Tape No. 118.

[3] Cannot locate source.

[4] *"A Second Chance"*, Billy Graham. More Stories for the Heart, Compiled by Alice Gray, Multnomah Publishers, 1997, p 37.

[5] *"'Cast Away': Thirst"*, Cast Away (Twentieth Century Fox, 2000); written by William Broyles Jr., directed by Robert Zemeckis; submitted by Bill White, Paramount, California. (Preachingtoday.com)

[6] *"Deer Addicted to Junk Food"*, Richard Young, Bossier City, Louisiana; Arkansas Democrat Gazette (Spring 1995). (Preachingtoday.com)

[7] *"Paralyzed by Things to Do"*, John Maxwell; Developing the Leader within You, (Thomas Nelson, 1993), p. 31; submitted by Eugene A. Maddox, Interlachen, Florida. (Preachingtoday.com)

[8] Charles Swindoll's Ultimate Book of Illustrations & Quotes, Charles R. Swindoll. (Thomas Nelson Publishers, 1998), p. 565.

[9] http://bibleforums.org/showthread.php?186569-In-Depth-Commentary-Book-of-James

[10] *"Trapped Bee Offers Simple Reminder on Temptation"*, Craig Brian Larson, editor of Preachingtoday.com

[11] *"Jump"*, Retold by Tania Gray. Stories for the Heart, Compiled by Alice Gray, Questar Publishers, 1996.

[12] Cannot locate source.

[13] Charles Swindoll's Ultimate Book of Illustrations & Quotes, Charles R. Swindoll. (Thomas Nelson Publishers, 1998), p. 446.

[14] *"Magic Factory Whistle"*, 1002 Humorous Illustrations for Public Speaking, Michael E. Hodgin, p. 28.

[15] "Transformed by an Elevator", Owen Bourgaize, Castel, Guernsey, United Kingdom. (preachingtoday.com)

[16] Cannot locate source.

[17] Cannot locate source.

[18] *"The Pests We Tolerate"*, Craig Brian Larson, editor of Preachingtoday.com; source: Anne R. Carey and Keith Simmons "Calling the Exterminators: Critters that bug us most", USA Today Snapshot (May 22-25), 1A; based on survey of 1,253 adults by Global Strategy Group for Orkin. (Preachingtoday.com)

[19] *"Man Forced to Clean Backyard"*, Brian Lowery and Brandon O'Brien, associate and assistant editors for PreachingToday.com; source: Associated Press, "Maryland Man Gets Jail Time for Junky Yard," www.abcnews.com (8-22-07). (Preachingtoday.com)

[20] *"We Still Have Value to God"*, Mike Silva, Would You Like Fries with That? (Word, 2005) Portland, Oregon. (Preachingtoday.com)

[21] *"Appearing on Baseball Card with Jesus"*, Shaun Brown, Newport News, Virginia. (Preachingtoday.com)

[22] *"Teen Brought Luggage to Her Baptism"*, Raymond McHenry, Stories for the Soul (Hendrickson, 2001), p. 48; submitted by Steve May, Humboldt, Tennessee. (preachingtoday.com)

[23] Charles Swindoll's Ultimate Book of Illustrations & Quotes, Charles R. Swindoll. (Thomas Nelson Publishers, 1998), p. 522.

[24] *Feeding the Wolves of the Heart"*, Author unknown; submitted by Bill White, Paramount, California. (Preachingtoday.com)

[25] *"Carl Sandburg on Human Nature"*, Richard Hansen, "A Good Mystery", Preaching Today Audio issue 253. (Preachingtoday.com)

[26] Cannot locate source.

[27] *"Daddy's Baby's Come Home"*, Jeannette Clift George, "Belonging and Becoming", Preaching Today, Tape No. 93. (Preachingtoday.com)

Need additional copies?

To order more copies of
Changed by the King's Presence,
contact NewBookPublishing.com

- ☐ Order online at NewBookPublishing.com
- ☐ Call 877-311-5100 or
- ☐ Email Info@NewBookPublishing.com

Call for multiple copy discounts!

Reliance Media

Additional Books by Kurt Litwiller

Living Out
The
Called Life
Running God's Race

New Covenant Living
Released to
Live by the Spirit

Humble King To
Conquering King
The Week That
Changed Everything

Order Your Copies Today!